bestofyear™

INTERIOR DESIGN BEST OF YEAR

EDITOR IN CHIEF
Cindy Allen

SENIOR EDITOR
Jen Renzi

SENIOR DESIGNER
Karla Lima

DESIGNERS
Zigeng Li
Giannina Macias

RESEARCH AND COPY
Annie Block
Kathryn Daniels
Jesse Dorris
Athena Waligore

CONTRIBUTING WRITERS
Craig Kellogg
Mark McMenamin
Stephen Treffinger

MANAGING EDITOR
Helene E. Oberman

PRODUCTION
Igor Tsiperson
Jessica Perrin
Sarah Dentry

BOOKS DIRECTOR
Selina Yee

MARKETING DIRECTOR
Tina Brennan

MARKETING ART DIRECTOR
Denise Figueroa

DIRECTOR OF MANUFACTURING AND DISTRIBUTION
Fern E. Meshulam

Library of Congress Control Number 2011922110
ISBN-13: 978-0-9833263-0-4
ISBN-10: 0-9833263-0-4

Printed in China
10 9 8 7 6 5 4 3 2 1

INTERIOR DESIGN®

INTERIOR DESIGN MAGAZINE
360 Park Avenue South, 17th Floor, New York, NY 10010 www.interiordesign.net

SANDOW | MEDIA™

SANDOW MEDIA LLC
Corporate Headquarters
3731 NW 8th Avenue, Boca Raton, FL 33431 www.sandowmedia.com

foreword by Cindy Allen

The idea of offering a yearly wide-angle view of the "best" design globally—intriguing me since the early days of my tenure as editor in chief of *Interior Design* magazine—finally became a concrete reality in 2006 with the launch of our Best of Year Awards. The panorama proved itself truly stunning and the numbers were staggering. Attracting over 1,200 project and product entries, the competition became an immediate, smashing success—and an ongoing testament to the vitality and creativity of the industry. Cumulatively, the winners and honorees represent an annual state of the union on design's cultural impact.

Now that our sixth year is well under way, we have finally found the necessary time and resources to make a substantial addition to the BoY Awards portfolio: Our inaugural book provides an official record of the most innovative designs that the commercial and residential realms offered in 2010. In keeping with the mission of the magazine, the work of emerging visionaries is showcased—and celebrated—alongside our industry's most venerated names. I am confident that this ad hoc directory of unequaled talent will serve not only as an inspiration for future entrants but also, more importantly, as a vital tool for any future client tasked with finding the perfect team to design its next award-winning project.

Bravo to all!

PROJECTS

best of year
contents

PRODUCTS

INDEX

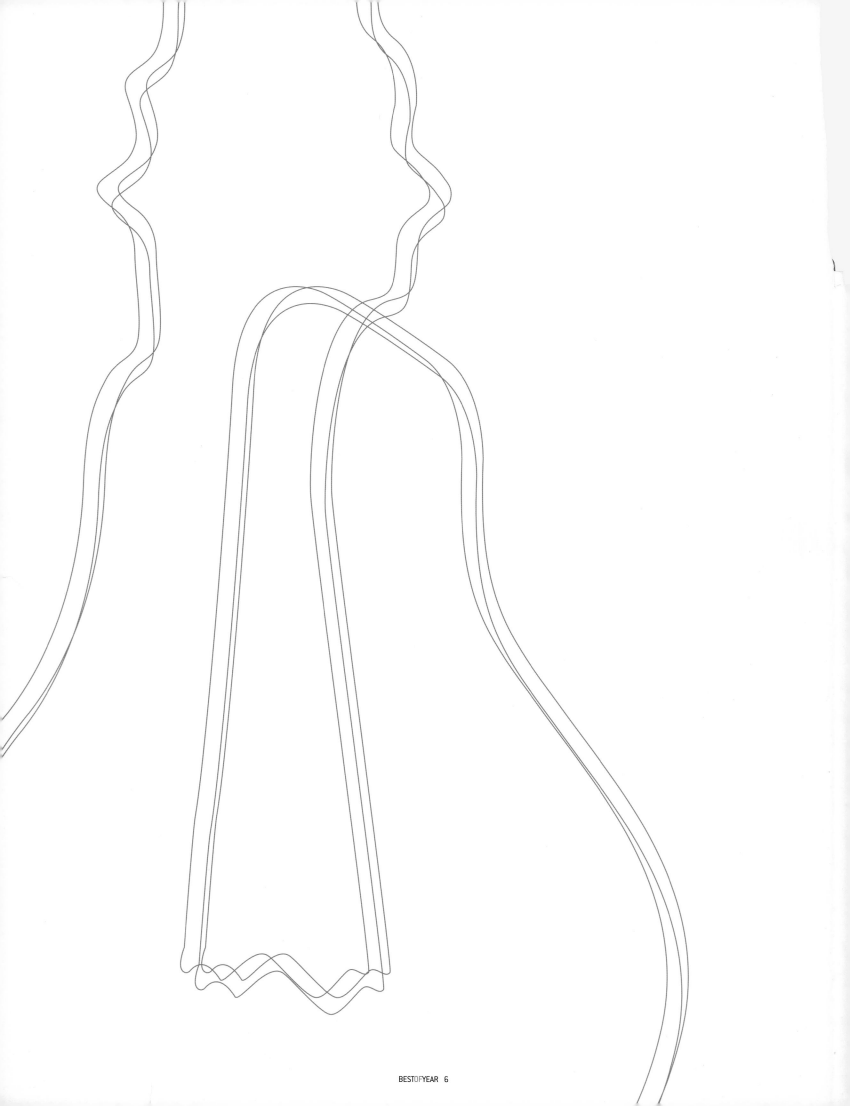

best of year

projects

RED BULL CANADA, TORONTO

Johnson Chou

WINNER BUDGET

Tapped to design the Toronto headquarters of Red Bull Canada, architect Johnson Chou created an office as stimulating as his client's elixir. And he did so on an exceedingly tight budget, leaving the building's industrial shell largely untouched and defining the space via sculptural interventions that read like art installations in a white-box gallery.

The scheme was fueled, Chou says, by the company's sponsorship of extreme sports and desire for the office to function as a cultural venue; thus the multitasking common areas, which double as hubs for exhibitions and events. The entry sequence establishes the buzzy vibe: A long red tube lit by color-shifting LEDs seduces visitors into reception, a loftlike space that can be reconfigured with pivoting wall panels. Beside it is a lounge area that the architect likens to an abstract cottage, lined with damask-print wallpaper and lit by a crystal chandelier.

In the double-height atrium beyond, a powder-coated steel staircase spirals to the upper level. Here, a swoop of painted gypsum-board encloses three meeting pods with walls that peel away to expose interiors lined in red vinyl or maple. Nearby is the staff lunchroom, with benches built from cherry to match the floor. Spotlighted by suspended fixtures of glass tubes encasing crystals, it's the perfect spot to kick back and drink up the high-energy design.

Clockwise from top left: A powder-coated steel spiral stairway leads through the atrium adjacent to reception. Above the lunchroom's custom granite table are halogen-lit glass pendant fixtures encasing crystals; the benches and floorboards are jatobá, a Brazilian cherry. The stair ascends to the upper level, where a steel walkway has frameless glass guards. ⬎

"I'm interested in surprise— the complexity within the simplicity"

A painted gypsum-board tunnel leading from the entry to reception encloses a hot-rolled-steel walkway—lit by LEDs—that culminates in a glowing frosted-glass platform. The lounge beside it is furnished with a crystal chandelier, a folding wooden chair, and a cowhide-covered drum table. ➤

1 EXECUTIVE OFFICES

2 ATRIUM

3 MEETING PODS

4 PRIVATE OFFICES

0 10 20   40

Clockwise from top left: *The curved structure housing the three meeting pods was originally built as a suite of recording studios for the Red Bull Music Academy. A pod's built-in banquette, visible through an acrylic window, is covered in faux rubber. In the first meeting pod, stools by Aúzamoliné line the bar of painted, polyurethaned MDF. Maple planks line two of the meeting pods, whose glass end walls frame a view of the Red Bull logo, rendered in electrical conduits.*

PROJECT TEAM SILKE STADTMUELLER; CAN BUI; HEATHER SHUTE

PHOTOGRAPHY TOM ARBAN

www.johnsonchou.com

AXIS DESIGN UNION

PROJECT Wanda International
Cinema, Hong Kong
STANDOUT Chinese red, this
cinema chain's corporate
color, plays a starring role in
the form of feature walls, LED
fixtures, and theater seats
PHOTOGRAPHY Kenchoifoto
www.axisdesignunion.com

CL3 ARCHITECTS

PROJECT CL3 Architects
office, Hong Kong
STANDOUT Using plywood
and sheet metal as well as
substituting curtains and
vintage sliding gates for
walls helped to keep costs
down at this open studio
PHOTOGRAPHY Nirut
Benjabanpot/CL3 Architects
www.cl3.com

LUNDBERG DESIGN

PROJECT Hourglass Blueline
Estate Winery, Calistoga,
California
STANDOUT At the entry
to a wine cave built into
the side of a hill, bottles
are embedded in a concrete
wall to let light filter through
PHOTOGRAPHY Ryan Hughes/
Lundberg Design
www.lundbergdesign.com

UNIVERSITY OF OREGON
JOHN E. JAQUA ACADEMIC CENTER
FOR STUDENT ATHLETES, EUGENE

ZGF Architects and Firm 151

WINNER EDUCATIONAL

This sleek student-athlete center is equal parts brain and brawn. Wrapped in a taut stainless-steel scrim that helps modulate interior temperature, the three-story glass box floats like a glacier on a pool of water. The 40,000-square-foot interior is a similar study in transparency, centering on a dramatic atrium enfolded by catwalks and overlooks.

The interiors, by ZGF Architects partner Gene Sandoval, overseen in collaboration with Firm 151 partner Randy Stegmeier, borrow from the playbook of hip hospitality design. To unify diverse spaces such as tutoring rooms, advising offices, computer labs, and auditoriums, the partners repeated materials and colors. White-oak millwork used for walls, floors, and furnishings lends the feel of a bento box. Undergrads do homework in traditional carrels or comfortable high-design seats, all upholstered in the school's signature lemon-yellow and emerald-green.

For all its slickness, the heart of the design is the scholars the facility serves, a sentiment the lobby's feature wall reflects. Upon close inspection, the pixilated mural of Albert Einstein turns out to be a collage of 10,000 stainless-steel squares, each etched with a student athlete's image.

Clockwise from top left: Patricia Urquiola's Malmö sofa occupies the ground-floor waiting lounge. Strips of white oak animate the walls of the three-story atrium. Stainless-steel scrim wraps the building's glass walls. ➤

Clockwise from top left: Near the study carrels stand a pair of Alfredo Häberli's Take a Line for a Walk chairs. Walled in low partitions of mirrored glass, a library slices through the atrium. A restroom is clad in glass mosaics. In the café on the lower level, sinuous custom sofas cluster around an open hearth. ➤

1 AUDITORIUM

2 HERITAGE SPACE

3 LIFE SKILLS

4 OFFICES

5 CONFERENCE ROOM

6 RESTROOM

7 TUTORING ROOMS

8 CAFÉ

0   20   40   80

WINNER **EDUCATIONAL**

Built on the site of a former parking lot, the center seems to float on a water table ringed by an enfilade of birch trees. ➤

"The design explores the limits of transparency and connectivity to provide a communal gathering and learning space"

—GENE SANDOVAL

Clockwise from opposite: Each "pixel" of the Einstein feature wall is a 3-by-3-inch stainless-steel etching of a University of Oregon student athlete. A scoreboard-style LED display behind an angular white-oak desk announces available tutoring appointments. Michel Ducaroy's Togo seats furnish the clubby student-athlete lounge.

PROJECT TEAMS BOB PACKARD; JAN WILLEMSE; ROBERT SNYDER; JENNIFER RUSSINA; WALKER TEMPLETON; YOSHIYUKI WATANABE; TRENT THELEN; MAN HUI CHAN; LARRY BRUTON; JOHN BRESHEARS; DINEKE KNIFFIN; RICH MOORE; ERICA RINELLA; LEE KILBORN; BRIAN STEVENS; RYAN THOMSON; ROBERT PETTY; JONAH ROSS (ZGF ARCHITECTS); JENN WARD (FIRM 151)

PHOTOGRAPHY BASIL CHILDERS (INTERIORS); RON COOPER (EXTERIORS)

www.zgf.com; www.firm151.com

1100: ARCHITECT

PROJECT New York University Department of Linguistics

STANDOUT Built-in seating upholstered in sunny colors updates a lounge's 19th-century cast-iron columns and exposed brick

PHOTOGRAPHY Michael Moran

www.1100architect.com

TSAO DESIGN GROUP

PROJECT Hult International Business School, San Francisco

STANDOUT A waffle slab floats above a lounge's seating by Ronan & Erwan Bouroullec and the adjacent glassed-in classroom

PHOTOGRAPHY David Wakely

www.tsaodesign.com

PERKINS + WILL

PROJECT New York University Leonard N. Stern School of Business

STANDOUT Set into a plaza's concrete pavement, panels of laminated glass bring sunlight into an atrium descending two levels belowground

PHOTOGRAPHY Eduard Hueber/Arch Photo

www.perkinswill.com

IA INTERIOR ARCHITECTS

PROJECT Collins College, Phoenix

STANDOUT Bold angles and saturated colors animate the interior of a concrete warehouse converted into classrooms and administrative offices

PHOTOGRAPHY Michael David Rose

www.interiorarchitects.com

BURGESS GROUP, ALEXANDRIA, VIRGINIA

Specializing in software for Medicare and Medicaid reimbursements, this company has earned LEED Platinum certification for a headquarters in a new building also by the SmithGroup. Extensive daylighting is among the many elements that added up to the U.S. Green Building Council's highest rating—on most days, sensors barely trigger the dimmable ballasts on the linear fixtures. In addition, associate Rob Moylan chose natural materials to convey authenticity and complexity. The desk in reception and the island in the pantry were both built with soapstone. Elm flooring was reclaimed from an old barn. Running along one side of the reception gallery that bisects the 17,000-square-foot floor plate, Vermont slate tiles cover an entire wall. And cork lines a break-out area. Throughout, color contrasts reflect and promote the duality of a company that's young yet stable, creative yet serious. Note the apple green and muted blue of the design lab's photomural, an abstracted image of Lyndon Johnson signing Medicare into law.

SmithGroup

WINNER GREEN

PROJECT TEAM ANDREW ROLLMAN; HOLLY HARSHMAN; PATRICK GREEN; PAUL HURT; CHRISTINE CLOWES
PHOTOGRAPHY ERIC LAIGNEL
www.smithgroup.com

RECOLOGY, SAN FRANCISCO

Rarely are salvaged maps and repurposed bicycle wheels considered building blocks of a business environment. Pollack Architecture principal David Galullo, however, put such detritus—and recycling itself—front and center when designing corporate headquarters for Recology, an employee-owned waste-removal company.

Some 68 employees work in the 20,000-square-foot office, which occupies a full floor of a downtown San Francisco high-rise. Sourcing furnishings and finishes for the decor was as easy as visiting Recology's local recycling plant, where the design team took an introductory tour and came away with both materials and inspiration. Through the client's decades-old artist-in-residence initiative, the designers met and subsequently collaborated with program alum Mike Farruggia to provide functional sculptures such as work surfaces constructed from resin-coated corrugated cardboard and conference room tables made with old street signs and computer motherboards.

Galullo estimates that his scheme for the new office includes more than 45 artworks, most exhibited in a gallery near reception. To highlight such pieces—not to mention the picture-postcard views of San Francisco's Bay Bridge—Galullo downplayed the architecture and maintained an earth-friendly ethos. Concrete counters incorporate fly ash, doors are re-harvested redwood, and backsplash tiles are made from coconut shells. For a recycling company that emphasizes leading by example, it comes as no surprise that the project received LEED Gold certification.

Pollack Architecture

HONOREE **GREEN**

Clockwise from top left: A table is topped with a patchwork of recycled street signs. The reception area, featuring a gypsum-board ceiling sheathed in rift cherry–veneer wall covering, is furnished with a coffee table collaged from repurposed castoffs. An executive office features scrap-material artworks and a credenza crafted from salvaged wood. ➤

Clockwise from left:
Animating a corridor is
a colorful installation
of squares cut from
the decks of
discarded skate-
boards. Recycled
children's bicycle
wheels were used to
create an occasional

table in an office.
A workstation is
crowned by a wall
hanging cobbled
together from
recycled tiles.

PROJECT TEAM CHRISTINE SHAW; JOELLE ROSANDER;
FEMIA DJOHAN; JENNIFER MCDONALD

PHOTOGRAPHY ERIC LAIGNEL

www.pollackarch.com

CHADA AND CIRCA ARCHITECTURE

PROJECT Saffire Freycinet, Coles Bay, Australia
STANDOUT This 20-key luxury resort's organic forms and plentiful use of stone and timber harmonize with the protected coastal landscape of the surrounding national park
PHOTOGRAPHY George Apostolidis
www.chada.com.au
www.circaarchitecture.com.au

MINARC

PROJECT House, Los Angeles
STANDOUT Instead of falling victim to the wrecking ball, more than half of a five-unit apartment building was preserved in converting it into a 3,850-square-foot single-family house
PHOTOGRAPHY David Lena
www.minarc.com

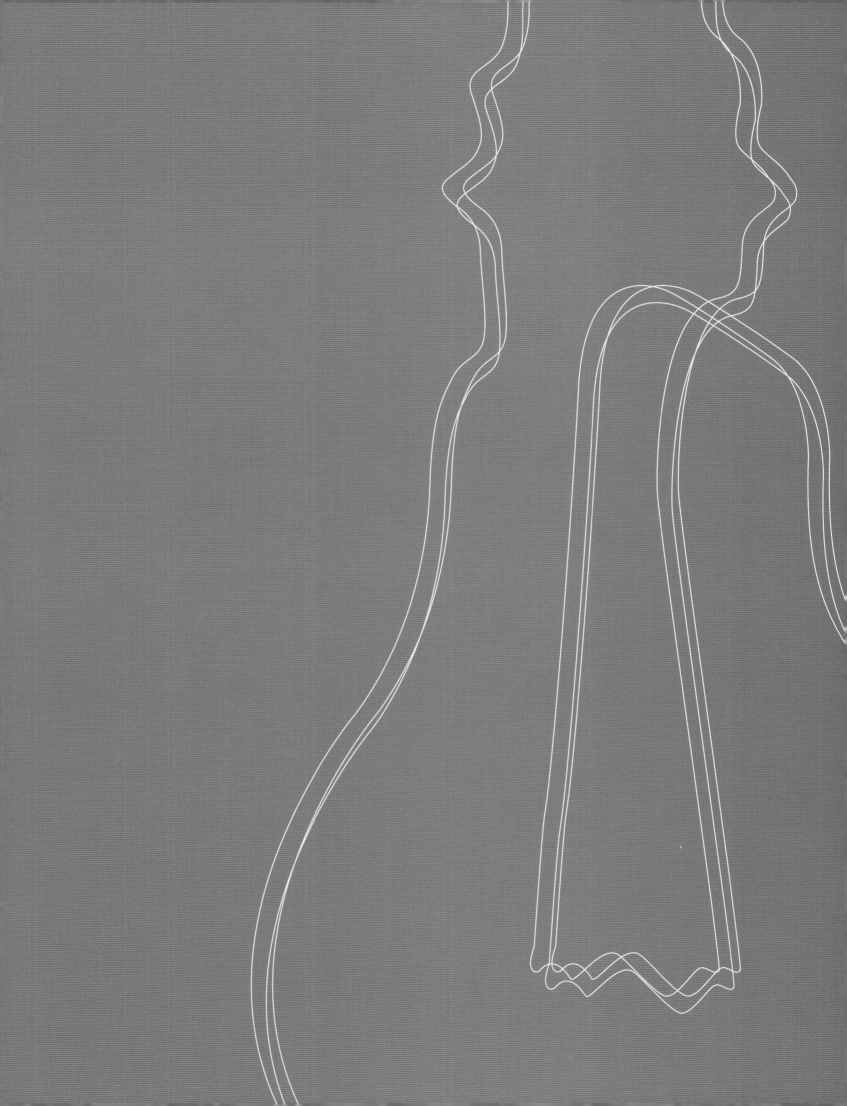

DUBAI MALL MEDICAL CENTRE, UNITED ARAB EMIRATES

Bloomingdale's and Giorgio Armani aren't the only major imports at the Burj Khalifa complex, formerly known as the Burj Dubai. In a building adjacent to the world's tallest tower, the Dubai Mall Medical Centre offers health care based on a Western model. The 60,000-square-foot project borrows such luxury-hospitality elements as sculptural furnishings and marble flooring. Taupe, pearlized cream, white, silver blue, and sea blue emerged as the color palette when senior associate Karen Miller Eskandari pixelated photographs of the region's landscape. Water, the ultimate desert luxury, became a metaphor in terms of both color and shape. Imagining how rain puddles, Eskandari used free-form carpet insets to anchor separate seating groups in the central waiting area. Semicircular ceiling tracks allow sheers, downlit by LEDs, to be pulled around each group for partial privacy. The sofas and ottomans she chose are round or curved in deference to Arabs' traditional flowing clothing, which is prone to snag on sharp corners. It's seating that would not appear at all out of place on the sales floor of Giorgio Armani.

NBBJ

WINNER HEALTH CARE / LARGE

Clockwise from far left: Polyester-cotton sheers, high-lighted by recessed LED fixtures, veil sections of the waiting area, where custom nylon carpet is set into flooring of local marble. Hall-ways and nurse stations have quartz floor tile. CNC-milled MDF backs the built-in MDF reception desk. In one seating group, custom chairs with leather seats surround a Frank Gehry–inspired table.

PROJECT TEAM JORGE NIEVES-RODRIGUEZ; KARSTEN BASTIEN; DENNIS BRANDON; LISA BAKER; BRUCE FARIS; MARK PERRY; MARK E. CROSS; STACIE SCHLABACH GILLILAND; CHIHARU SATO; EARL LEE; TIM BREWSTER JONES; TOM FOX; MARY BUTENSCHON; TIM LAI; MICHAEL DENISON; ALI UZUN

PHOTOGRAPHY TIM GRIFFITH

www.nbbj.com

Karim Rashid

WINNER HEALTH CARE / SMALL

OASIS OF HEALTH, BELGRADE, SERBIA

Walking around Belgrade, you might pass a dozen Oasis of Health pharmacies. Most are re-creations of antiquated apothecaries, complete with dark paneling. The latest one, however, is the singular vision of *Interior Design* Hall of Fame member Karim Rashid. Because the 480-square-foot space was previously accessible only through the lobby of this 1950's building, he had to break through the travertine facade to create a street entrance, then build stairs to bridge the 4½-foot gap between the sidewalk and the floor level inside. Balustrades are the Oasis of Health logo's kelly green, as is the cash-wrap desk straight ahead. The desk is shaped like a jelly bean and mounted so that the bottom appears to rest lightly on the vine leaves of the logo, printed on ceramic floor tiles. Built-in vitrines display pills and potions. Pulsing across the center of the ceiling, a double helix of LEDs recalls a patient's healthy heartbeat on an EKG monitor.

Clockwise from left:
Rashid broke through the building's facade to add a street entrance, bridging the difference in level with a flight of stairs with pink treads. Druggists stand behind a gel-coated desk shaped like a jelly bean. Ceramic floor tiles are printed with the vine leaves of the Oasis of Health logo. A double helix of digitally animated LEDs pulses across the ceiling.

PROJECT TEAM CAMILA TARIKI; JULIE HYUNJU LEE

PHOTOGRAPHY BRANKO STARČEVIĆ

www.karimrashid.com

SPARC, SAN FRANCISCO

Sand Studios

HONOREE HEALTH CARE

Like the produce counter at a Whole Foods market, SPARC is a gourmet purveyor of artisanal consumables. The main difference is that the product sold at this San Francisco dispensary could get you arrested in many states: medical marijuana. Designed by principal Larissa Sand, the nonprofit San Francisco Patient Resource Center offers a range of health services as well as lab-tested cannabis grown by members of an area collective. To preserve shoppers' privacy—while still admitting sunlight—Sand enlivened the storefront with a syncopated hopscotch of translucent watery-blue panes and etched glass that veil the dealings inside.

Sand's design for the 2,000-square-foot retail area builds on the industrial bones of the site, a former warehouse. She cites the Zen spirit of Japanese tearooms and the shelving systems of old-school apothecary shops as inspirations. Instead of using heavy antique-style woodwork for display, however, she floated her system on steel scaffolding hung on aged-concrete walls. The cannabis is stored in dovetailed oak bins accessed from a rolling steel ladder.

For environmental and economic reasons, the metal used incorporates more than 70 percent recycled content, and the concrete counters were sourced nearby. Eco-certified oak also salvaged locally forms countertops inset with custom science-glass dishes stashing cannabis buds. Throughout, care and craftsmanship with simple materials helped Sand achieve principles of conservation, thrift, and social responsibility.

PROJECT TEAM TRAVIS HAYES; BEN DAMRON;
ALAN DOUGHERTY; ANDREW LIEBERMAN
PHOTOGRAPHY KEN PROBST

www.sandstudios.com

Clockwise from top left: Frosted heat-resistant glass pendants and a polished concrete floor enliven the medical marijuana dispensary. Seen from within, the custom facade incorporates a patchwork of translucent glass panels. Marijuana storage boxes and cannabis seedlings in trays hang from a recycled-metal display structure. The cubistic frosted-glass storefront floats on a concrete plinth imprinted with formwork to complement the wood-plank facade.

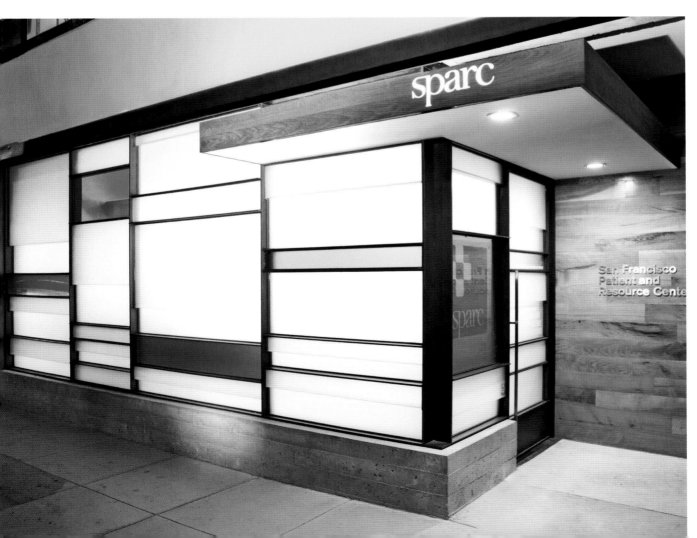

NBBJ

PROJECT Seattle Children's Hospital, Bellevue, Washington
STANDOUT Extensive glass brings sunlight and views into corridors, waiting areas, and patient-care facilities at this satellite clinic
PHOTOGRAPHY Benjamin Benschneider
www.nbbj.com

PAGE SOUTHERLAND PAGE

PROJECT Chickasaw Nation Medical Center, Ada, Oklahoma
STANDOUT A deep connection to the natural environment comes through in such materials as fieldstone, oxidized copper, and ipe
PHOTOGRAPHY Art Gray
www.pspaec.com

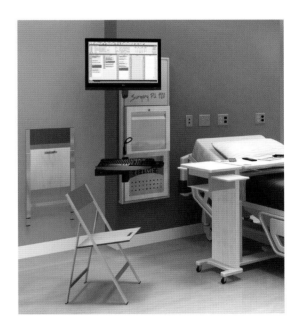

Patricia Urquiola

WINNER HOTEL

A prolific furniture designer makes her hotel debut with a
five-star chain's first Spanish location. (It's on the storied
Passeig de Gràcia—Antoni Gaudí's Casa Batlló apartments
are just steps away.) Partnering with Ferrater & Asociados
and Juan Trias de Bes TDB Arquitectura, Patricia Urquiola
handled virtually every aspect of the interiors. The result
is a singular interpretation of understated luxury. Eastern
details, evoking Mandarin Oriental's Hong Kong heritage,
are filtered through a Western prism. In the formal
restaurant, abstracted flowers bloom on the orange silk
carpet, complemented by clouds gold-leafed on sections
of the ceiling. She also played with the concept of Asian
screens, suspending geometric white PVC versions in the
skylit double-height lounge, then repeating the motif on the
acoustical wall covering. In the 98 guest rooms, shiny white
wardrobes are meant to resemble Japanese lacquered
boxes. Asia aside, it's pure Urquiola: from sofas and stools
to beds and benches.

*Clockwise from
above: Urquiola's
chaise longues line
the iroko decking
around the spa's
granite-clad lap pool.
In the lobby lounge,
a suspended PVC
screen's geometric
motif repeats on the
acoustical wall
covering behind.
The steel doors of
safe-deposit boxes
cover the ceiling and
walls of the bar. The
formal restaurant
features Urquiola
armchairs and a gold-
leafed ceiling. Above
the oak concierge
desk, a mirrored
ceiling reflects an
anodized-aluminum
screen and Achille
Castiglioni lamp.*

PROJECT TEAM RODRIGO IZQUIERDO; CRISTINA BÁRCENAS
PHOTOGRAPHY ERIC LAIGNEL
www.patriciaurquiola.com

CL3 Architects

HONOREE HOTEL

EAST, HONG KONG

A certain kind of guest might be persuaded to curl up in the groovy Eero Aarnio Bubble seat hanging in a suite at the East hotel in Hong Kong. But what to make of Mainland sculptor Sui Jianguo's fuchsia resin Tyrannosaurus roaring beside it? Credit these and other unexpected touches to firm principal William Lim, who designed the playful 32-floor property as a flagship for Swire Pacific's fledgling brand of innovative "business hotels with a life."

Throughout, Lim balanced an offbeat sensibility with businesslike pragmatism. For instance, the 345 guest rooms eschew the typical shoebox shape, which would have limited window exposure to the short end. Instead, most are more squared off to emphasize glazing—a 16-foot expanse—facing Victoria Harbour. Also enhancing the illusion of spaciousness in the snug quarters are streamlined furnishings, a restrained materials palette, and free flow between bathroom and sleeping area; only the shower and toilet are enclosed.

The hotel's serene backdrop of limestone, walnut, and limed elm is punctuated by lively artworks. Above the cantilevered reception desk glows a digitally printed, backlit vinyl landscape by Hong Kong's Marc & Chantal Design. Sculptor Jayne Dyer's installation of orange-painted steel butterflies takes flight in the casual eatery Feast. Perhaps most dramatic is the grand staircase: Its crisscross timber elements recall Herzog & de Meuron's "bird's nest" stadium 1,200 miles away in Beijing.

Clockwise from top left: *The East hotel entry is marked by walnut and limed elm. In the lobby, a 32-foot-long stretch of internally lit solid-surfacing forms the reception desk. A glass balustrade and treads showcase the grand staircase, composed of timber and blackened stainless steel.* ➤

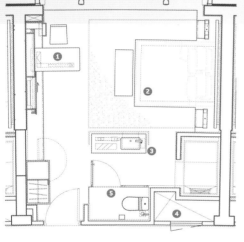

1 DESK

2 SLEEPING AREA

3 SINK

4 SHOWER

5 WC

0   2.5   5   10

Clockwise from top left: *Guest suites pair limed-elm woodwork and Rio white limestone floors with Eero Aarnio Bubble chairs and Sui Jianguo's resin Tyrannosaurus sculptures. Airy all-day dining is available at the second-floor restaurant Feast, where optical film spells out the hotel name on the windows. To energize the wall surfaces over the beds in the open-plan guest rooms, Lim applied vinyl sheets printed with black-and-white photos.* ➤

"Playful artwork is a bit unusual in a business-hotel setting"

Above the bar at Feast, Jayne Dyer's painted-steel butterfly sculptures float on vinyl-wrapped plywood panels. ➤

Clockwise from left:
The stairway, with reception artwork by Marc & Chantal Design, can be seen from the street. The stairs lead to the restaurant Feast. The floor of Sugar, the penthouse bar, casts a surreal glow via laminated glass panels underlit by LEDs.

PROJECT TEAM RAYMOND CHOW
PHOTOGRAPHY NIRUT BENJABANPOT/CL3 ARCHITECTS
www.cl3.com

YABU PUSHELBERG

PROJECT St. Regis Mexico City

STANDOUT A series of intimate rooms furnished with rich colors and textures, the public spaces feel like a lavish home

PHOTOGRAPHY Evan Dion

www.yabupushelberg.com

MARKZEFF

PROJECT Hard Rock Hotel & Casino, Las Vegas

STANDOUT Celebrity-driven artwork, graphic wallpaper, and oversize furniture are designed to appeal to the club kid and business executive alike

PHOTOGRAPHY Eric Laignel

www.markzeff.com

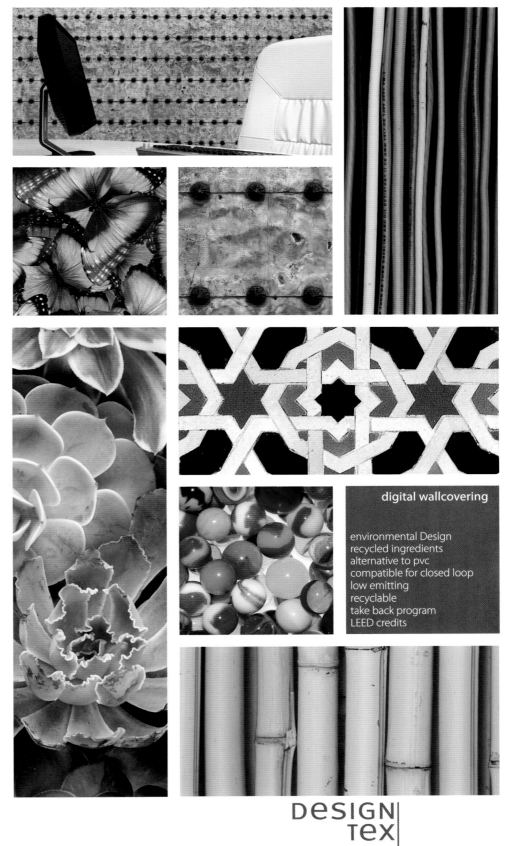

digital wallcovering

environmental Design
recycled ingredients
alternative to pvc
compatible for closed loop
low emitting
recyclable
take back program
LEED credits

DESIGN TEX
digital RINEKWALL

Neri & Hu
Design
and
Research
Office

WINNER HOTEL RENOVATION

WATERHOUSE AT SOUTH BUND, SHANGHAI, CHINA

Past and present coalesce thoughtfully at a 1930's Japanese army headquarters transformed into a boutique property by the husband-wife team of Lyndon Neri and Rossana Hu. The architects restored the original building—notably its brick and concrete walls and interior balconies—then added a fourth story wrapped in Cor-Ten steel. Also used for the front entry, this industrial material is a nod to the history of the city's Haungpu River docks. More polished are the furnishings inside the hotel, most of them familiar to customers of Neri and Hu's nearby gallery, Design Republic. A gleaming white-lacquered chandelier by Studio Job hangs in the triple-height reception area, and the 19 oak-floored guest rooms feature seating by Jean Prouvé, Charles and Ray Eames, and Bertjan Pot and Marcel Wanders. In some of the rooms, bathtubs take center stage, enclosed only by a transparent box of tinted glass.

Clockwise from left:
The courtyard's recycled-wood shutters are mirror-backed. Visitors enter through the concrete 1930's army building. Guest rooms feature glass-enclosed Duravit tubs. Guests dine at recycled-wood custom refrectory tables in the brick-floored restaurant. A custom concrete check-in counter and lacquered paper-mâché chandelier animate the main reception area.

PROJECT TEAM DEBBY HAEPERS; CAI CHUN YAN; MARKUS STOECKLEIN; JANE WANG; DAGMAR NIECKE; BRIAR HICKLING; CHRISTINE NERI; VIVI LAU; YANG SU; BRIAN LO; YUN ZHAO

PHOTOGRAPHY PEDRO PEGENAUTE; DERRYCK MENERE

www.nhdro.com

FRIDA ESCOBEDO AND **JOSÉ ROJAS**

PROJECT Hotel Boca Chica, Acapulco, Mexico

STANDOUT With its retro furnishings, painted steel signage, and mosaic murals, this 1950's hotel looks as if it hasn't changed a bit since its jet-set heyday

PHOTOGRAPHY Undine Pröhl

www.grupohabita.mx

ROTTET STUDIO

PROJECT Surrey, New York

STANDOUT This rejuvenated beaux arts landmark from 1925 now oozes sophistication, like a posh pied-à-terre with progressive artwork

PHOTOGRAPHY Eric Laignel

www.rottetstudio.com

CHAMPALIMAUD   **PROJECT** Fairmont San Francisco

STANDOUT Atop a 1907 building, a deco-era penthouse addition features a library rotunda, a dining room that can accommodate 60, and a lithograph by David Hockney

PHOTOGRAPHY Matthew Millman

www.champalimauddesign.com

SAFFIRE FREYCINET, COLES BAY, AUSTRALIA

The creative team behind this resort didn't have to look far for inspiration. Located on the east coast of Tasmania's Freycinet Peninsula, the property sits adjacent to undeveloped protected land and boasts jaw-dropping views of Coles Bay and the Hazards mountain chain. Moreover, the resort hugs a gentle curve of sandy shoreline near a spot where migrating whales and dolphins come to play. The luxury retreat's eco-minded buildings, by Circa Architecture director Peter Walker, and interiors, the work of Chada creative director Juliet Ashworth, recall the stunning natural surroundings. The rippling sapphire-blue water, flowing white dunes, gray-green bushland, and pink granite peaks were translated into an edited, cohesive palette of finishes that integrates the indoors and out.

Particularly organic is the main pavilion's roofline, crafted from local timber. The slanted roofs of the 20 freestanding suites—featuring full-height glass walls—combine to create a rippling wave effect. Though they nod to the land, the structures tread lightly on it: High-performance glass conserves energy while subdued inner and outer lighting ensures that the resort has minimal visual impact on the landscape after dark.

Chada and Circa Architecture

WINNER HOTEL / RESORT

"A strong element of the brief was that guests could sit in bed and take in the view"

—PETER WALKER

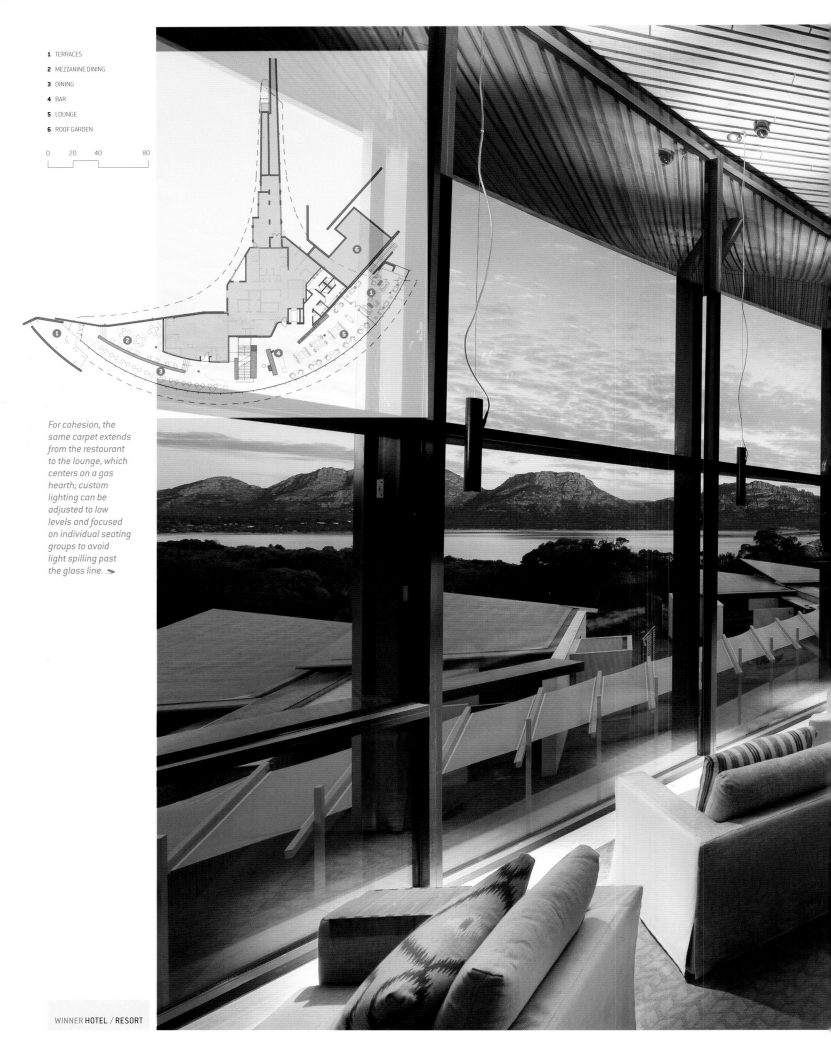

1 TERRACES
2 MEZZANINE DINING
3 DINING
4 BAR
5 LOUNGE
6 ROOF GARDEN

0   20   40   80

For cohesion, the
same carpet extends
from the restaurant
to the lounge, which
centers on a gas
hearth; custom
lighting can be
adjusted to low
levels and focused
on individual seating
groups to avoid
light spilling past
the glass line. ⬎

WINNER HOTEL / RESORT

Clockwise from top left: *The main pavilion sits upslope from the 20 suites. A freestanding stone-composite custom tub animates the Spa Saffire, which is floored in Shima Chiaro marble. The spa's lounge area boasts a Blackheart sassafras coffee table made by local joiners; the custom exterior lighting, by Point of View, was designed to represent reeds in the water. Bathrooms feature walls of the same Shima Chiaro marble plus glass-enclosed showers with views of private Zen courtyards.*

PROJECT TEAMS MICHAEL WATSON; KRISTI WAYMAN (CHADA); POPPY TAYLOR; JARROD HUGHES; ROBERT MORRIS-NUNN; GANCHE CHAU; CHRIS ROBERTS; GARY FLEMING; TINA CURTIS; JUDI DAVIS (CIRCA ARCHITECTURE)

PHOTOGRAPHY GEORGE APOSTOLIDIS

www.chada.com.au; www.circaarchitecture.com.au

NARADA VILLA & SPA RESORT, SANYA, CHINA

PAL Design Consultants

HONOREE HOTEL / RESORT

One word—paradise—sums up what PAL Design Consultants sought to conjure in this resort, an ultraluxury property in China's southernmost city, Sanya. And nothing says paradise quite like fanciful tropical blooms, reasoned firm principal Patrick Leung and senior designer Doris Chiu.

As it happens, the crane flower (perhaps better known as the bird-of-paradise), with its spiky orange and purplish petals atop a long slender stem, is considered auspicious in this part of Asia. Thus this shapely bloom, a symbol of happiness, became the resort's motif. In the atrium lobby, a wall with backlit blossom cutouts forms the backdrop for a spectacular double-height crystal sculpture. The flower's likeness is also projected onto walls of the Chinese fine-dining restaurant. And the distinctive silhouette is die-cut into the wood-veneer shades of light fixtures in guest-suite bathrooms and sitting areas.

Other elements unify the property's 100,000-square-foot interiors. Public spaces feature an exotic palette of marble, *merbau* woodwork, and lavastone wall treatments. Water features lend cohesion as well as serenity: The aforementioned sculpture hangs above a shallow reflecting pool, while a second pond extends from the building's rear facade toward the ocean beyond. Paradise, indeed.

Clockwise from far left: A reflecting pool extends from the hotel's rear. The lobby, with a marble floor and merbau beam ceiling, features a crystal sculpture suspended over a reflecting pool. At the property's Chinese fine-dining restaurant, merbau latticework columns flank a console table. Wood-veneer box shades die-cut with crane flowers hang above a guest room's double vanity. A foyer in the conference building features weather-resistant seating.

PHOTOGRAPHY BAO SZE WANG

www.paldesign.cn

HBA/HIRSCH BEDNER ASSOCIATES

PROJECT Four Seasons Resort Seychelles
STANDOUT Perched on a jungle hillside, most
of the 67 villas are tree houses, built on stilts
and furnished in a Creole style
PHOTOGRAPHY Peter Mealin
www.hbadesign.com

HBA/HIRSCH BEDNER ASSOCIATES

PROJECT Qasr Al Sarab, Abu Dhabi, United Arab Emirates
STANDOUT Traditional elements include the hammam's
heated marble treatment platform and the library's
antiqued-bronze lanterns
PHOTOGRAPHY Durston Saylor
www.hbadesign.com

Isay Weinfeld

WINNER BAR / LOUNGE

NUMERO, SÃO PAULO, BRAZIL

Clockwise from left:
The main hall features
13 reissued wall
lamps by industrial
designer Robert
Dudley Best. Blue
marine limestone
stairs ascend an ipe-
paneled stairwell
inset with banisters.
The facade's numeral
blocks are laser-cut
from marine plywood.
A private function
lounge downstairs
has walls papered
in poster fragments.

Numerical typesetting blocks, supersized in laser-cut marine plywood resin-coated in dark colors, announce this lounge in the city's ritzy Jardins district. From a front garden planted with tropical grasses, a sound track of bossa nova and alternative rock lures patrons up a stainless-steel ramp that extends into a long entry lined in bronze-coated mirror. This tunnellike procession deposits them in a small vestibule where two choices emerge. Proceed straight ahead, where leather-covered sofas and stools and galvanized-steel tables and ottomans furnish a moodily lit lounge that steps down in sections, under a gray-carpeted ceiling that continually rises. Or take the limestone stairs down to the private room. Here, color-changing LEDs, recessed in round ceiling cutouts, cast a glow on sidewalls papered with a collage of vintage poster fragments—and caipirinhas wash down tuna tartare. Both levels terminate at window walls facing a back garden—a paradise of jasmine, orchids, and palms.

PROJECT TEAM DOMINGOS PASCALI; MARCELO ALVARENGA;
MONICA CAPPA SANTONI; ALEXANDRE NOBRE; JULIANA GARCIA

PHOTOGRAPHY LEONARDO FINOTTI

www.isayweinfeld.com

ELLIOTT + ASSOCIATES ARCHITECTS

PROJECT Republic Gastropub, Oklahoma City

STANDOUT Flat-screen TVs are the only standard fare in a sports bar with coated-glass "bubble walls" and a terrazzo floor, sheltered by a sharply cantilevered roof

PHOTOGRAPHY Scott McDonald/Hedrich Blessing

www.e-a-a.com

ICRAVE

PROJECT Colony, Los Angeles

STANDOUT The lifeguard stand out front announces this nightclub's Hamptons beach theme, picked up by the mural in the boutique nook selling the work of artists and designers

PHOTOGRAPHY John Ellis

www.icravedesign.com

ROTTET STUDIO

PROJECT Bar Pleiades, New York

STANDOUT In the Surrey hotel, a black-and-white lacquered wall and tufted faux-suede upholstery reference Chanel makeup compacts and handbags

PHOTOGRAPHY Tom McWilliam

www.rottetstudio.com

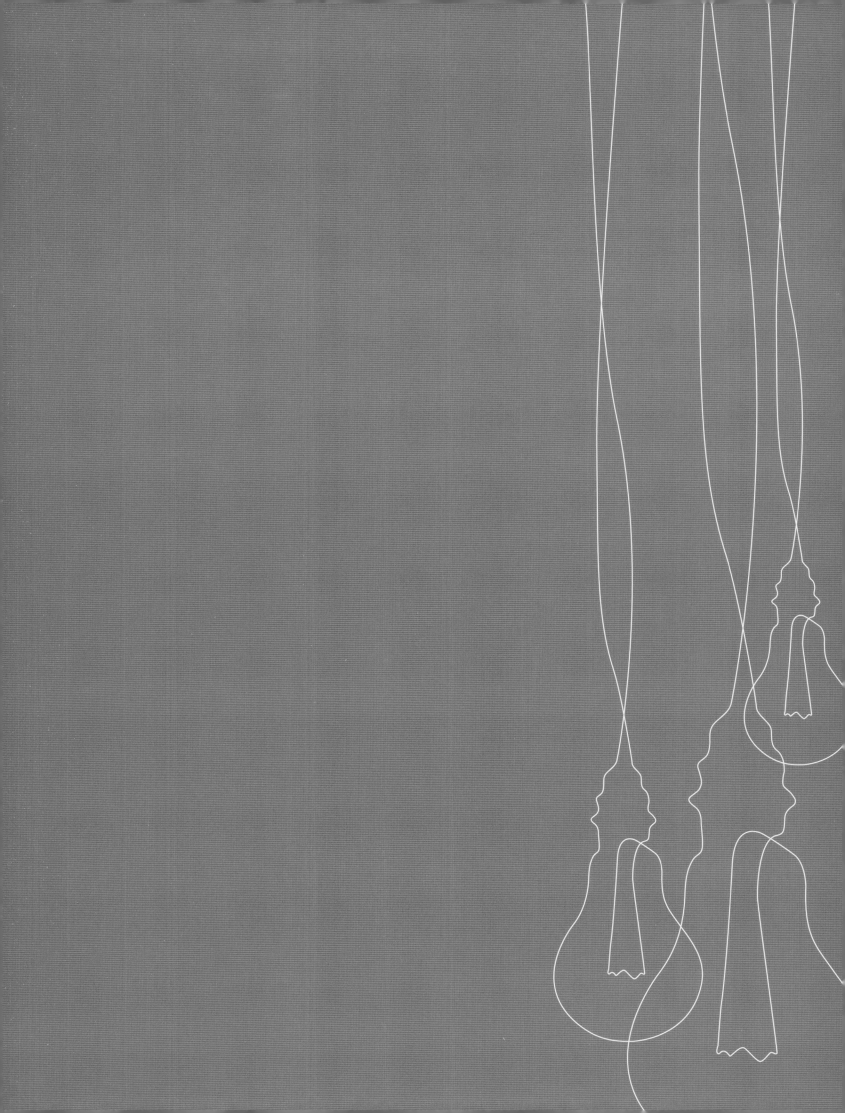

KUBRICK CAFÉ, BEIJING, CHINA

For anyone with Stanley Kubrick's love of history and obsessive research—think *Spartacus, Barry Lyndon,* and *Full Metal Jacket*—this particular story starts in Hong Kong, with the original Kubrick Bookshop. Principals Ajax Law Ling Kit and Virginia Lung maintained its laid-back charm in Beijing when designing not only a satellite location but also a spin-off, the book-centric Kubrick Café. Both are at Steven Holl Architects's massive mixed-used Linked Hybrid complex. Its eight towers, connected by sky bridges, inspired the architectural quality of the 37,000-square-foot café's display fixtures, variously sized steel boxes powder-coated green in honor of the leafy trees that eventually become paper for books. Another Beijing reference, the power lines looping through the streets, inspired the skeins of lamp cord terminating with extra-large incandescent bulbs. Above the café tables, illumination spills from an army of oversize black swing-arm task lamps bolted to the ceiling or a teak feature wall.

One Plus Partnership
WINNER CAFÉ

PHOTOGRAPHY AJAX LAW LING KIT AND VIRGINIA LUNG/
ONE PLUS PARTNERSHIP
www.onepluspartnership.com

Clockwise from far left: *Movie previews are shown on a pair of LCD screens inset into the teak wall. Custom display modules of powder-coated steel are screwed together to create a retail landscape that reconfigures readily. Steven Holl Architects chose granite flooring for every building in the Linked Hybrid complex. Painted plastic-covered lamp cord powers 75-watt halogen lightbulbs, dimmed for the proper ambience.*

CADENA ASOCIADOS AND ESRAWE STUDIO

PROJECT Cielito Querido Café, Mexico City

STANDOUT Bold colors and graphic patterns contrast with dark timber, giving Latin American café culture a neo-retro spin

PHOTOGRAPHY Jaime Navarro

www.cadena-asociados.com

www.esrawe.com

MOSCHELLA + ROBERTS

PROJECT Uptown Cafeteria and Support Group, Minneapolis

STANDOUT Riffing on the mid-century diner, hundreds of plastic lunch trays surface a corridor, while wood-grain plastic laminate frames the vinyl-covered booths

PHOTOGRAPHY John Abernathy

www.moschellaroberts.com

HOK **PROJECT** Green Grind, Toronto

STANDOUT Vintage furnishings bring a laid-back vibe to this eco-friendly coffee shop near the University of Toronto—ditto for the bicycle wheels on the wall

PHOTOGRAPHY Tom Arban

www.hok.com

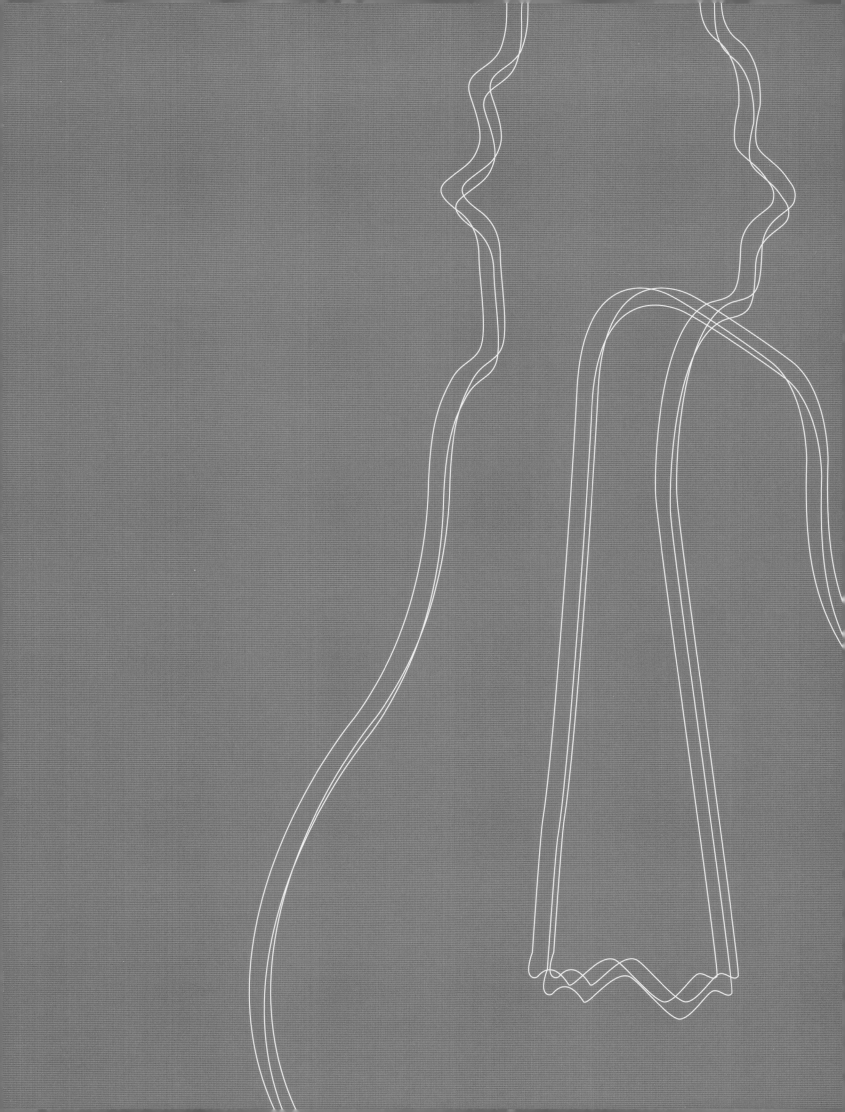

THE WRIGHT, NEW YORK

Andre Kikoski Architect

WINNER RESTAURANT

Andre Kikoski had already completed several notable eateries when The Wright at the Solomon R. Guggenheim Museum cemented the verdict: His name became officially synonymous with haute hospitality. Shortly after its opening, the restaurant proved *the* hot topic on many a culture Web site—and among the culturati. Driving further interest is a site-specific installation by sculptor Liam Gillick, a friend of the architect's.

Kikoski received the commission—part of the Guggenheim's 50th-anniversary celebration—at the same time he was tapped to complete an espresso bar in the museum's rotunda. In both projects, the challenge was to reference Frank Lloyd Wright's iconic spiral without being slavish. His vision for the 1,600-square-foot ground-floor space is suitably sinuous, with stacked curves that hug the walls and ceiling. Kikoski accommodated 58 diners within the snug footprint by pushing design elements to the perimeter, such as the ceiling's stretched fabric and the laminated-walnut paneling behind the bar. Gallerylike white walls and resin flooring set off the autumnal tones of Gillick's sculpture, called *The Horizon Produced by a Factory Once It Had Stopped Producing Views.* Now part of the museum's collection, the piece is modular and can be reinstalled elsewhere should Kikoski ever get called back for a fresher-upper.

Clockwise from top left: A stretched ceiling system created the triple-boomerang effect of the above-bar canopy. Sculptor Liam Gillick's installation, made of powder-coated-aluminum planks, screens interior storefront windows original to the Frank Lloyd Wright design. A banquette is upholstered in leather and polyester. ➤

PROJECT TEAM BRIAN LEWIS; GUNNAR JUNG; ADAM DARTER;
LIAM HARRIS; CLAIRE FOY; LAURIE KARSTEN
PHOTOGRAPHY PETER AARON/ESTO

www.akarch.com

Clockwise from left:
The curves of the bar-height communal dining table echo the sculptured ceiling. Tracing parallel tracks across the back bar's concave walnut paneling, internal fiber optics and LEDs light up translucent glass shelves. The swooping forms recall the signature spiral of the museum rotunda.

ELLIOTT + ASSOCIATES ARCHITECTS

PROJECT Elements, Oklahoma City

STANDOUT On the Chesapeake Energy Corporation campus, a tower built from steel louvers marks the entry to a staff restaurant with fiber-optic "fireflies" in the dining area

PHOTOGRAPHY Scott McDonald/Hedrich Blessing

www.e-a-a.com

GRAFT

PROJECT Breeze Café, Las Vegas

STANDOUT At CityCenter's Aria Resort & Casino, undulating forms overhead define poolside dining and lounging areas unified by a materials palette of stucco and Brazilian redwood

PHOTOGRAPHY Ricky Ridecós

www.graftlab.com

ICRAVE

PROJECT Collective, New York

STANDOUT An 11-person team of artists and artisans spent three months turning second-hand finds and other bargain items into ingenious seating, tables, and lighting

PHOTOGRAPHY Eric Laignel

www.icravedesign.com

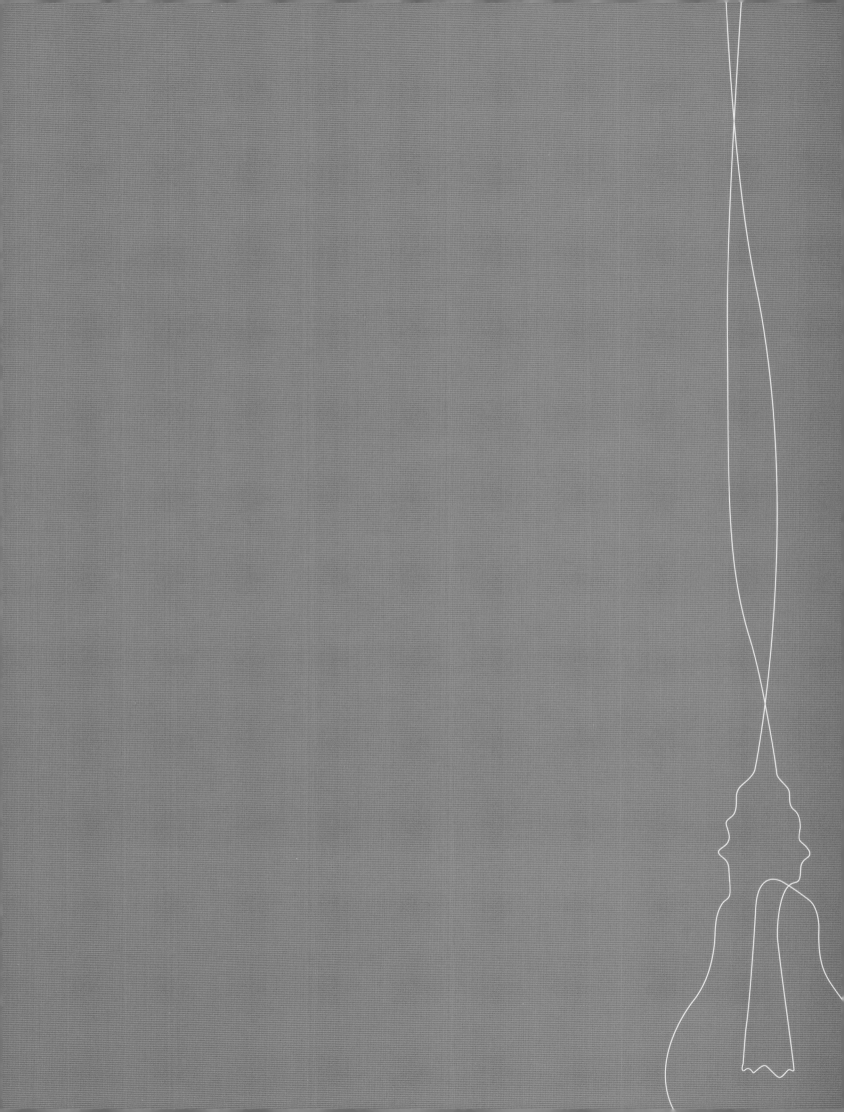

A symphony of shiny surfaces and multicolored lights, Simone Micheli says, transports the Boscolo Exedra Milano hotel's 5,400-square-foot spa to another dimension, "one that's surreal, metaphysical, and unlikely." He dotted the ceiling in the reception area and the corridors with half-bubbles of chromium-plated plastic, then went all out clustering hundreds around and above the pool for a kaleidoscopic effect. Below the surface of the water, white LEDs illuminate hydro-massage jets. Poolside, four showers are lit with red or blue LEDs, indicating warm or cold water. The fantasy continues nearby with virtual landscapes projected on a wall behind a row of white daybeds. Beyond the pool, spa-goers discover a cedar-paneled sauna, a mosaic-tiled Turkish bath, and six treatment rooms lined with chartreuse lacquered cabinets.

Simone Micheli Architectural Hero

WINNER SPA

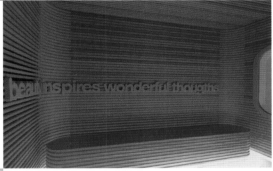

Clockwise from far left: Landscape scenes are projected onto an accent wall behind the daybeds, upholstered in eco-friendly leather. The chromium-plated plastic bubbles first appear on the ceiling in reception. An inspirational quote wraps around two walls of the cedar-lined sauna. Treatment rooms feature minimalist massage tables and colorful lacquered storage walls. The bubbles reappear above the pool, which is lit by LEDs.

PHOTOGRAPHY JÜRGEN EHEIM

www.simonemicheli.com

Jiun Ho

HONOREE **SPA**

REVEL SPA, SAN FRANCISCO

Avian details lift your spirits the moment you step inside San Francisco's Revel Spa. A flock of birdcages that designer Jiun Ho found in Thailand cluster overhead. The reception desk below also seems to take flight, resting on just a narrow pedestal. And winged sculptures flutter across a wall in the lower-level waiting area. Such elements suggest that the weight of the real world is of no concern here; levity and relaxation are the main attractions.

Principles of feng shui and keeping-things-simple helped Ho limit the budget and minimize environmental impact. A stream of water cascades through the center of the staircase and into a gold-leafed urn. Ethereal touches such as white scrims are anchored by heartier materials like the weathered oak planks that cover the reception desk, fill a void in the dropped ceiling above the cages, and crisscross below pipes and ductwork in the nail salon, where they fold down to form manicure stations. The en-suite restroom of the largest treatment room is lined in antique teak panels salvaged from the remains an old Thai house. Ho reinforced the Eastern mood with his own framed photographs of Vietnamese landscapes. To a spa-goer gazing at the images of mysterious mountains and placid seas, achieving nirvana almost seems possible.

Clockwise from top left: Salvaged teak paneling clads a treatment room's restroom. Ho photographed the spa's series of framed Asian landscapes. In reception, antique Thai birdcages dangle from reclaimed oak planks that hide pipes and ductwork. ➤

PROJECT TEAM JENN RADLINSKI

PHOTOGRAPHY BRUCE DAMONTE

www.jiunho.com

Clockwise from far left: A stair in concrete, laminated glass, and steel leads down to treatment areas. Wool flannel sheathes two walls of a treatment room. George Nelson chairs face a Burmese Buddha and an oak cabinet housing nail dryers. Wide oak

planks form the manicure stations. Polyester curtains separate the pedicure stations in the nail salon, floored in epoxy resin.

HONOREE SPA

UNITED DESIGNERS

PROJECT Bliss, Doha, Qatar
STANDOUT With the honeycomb of hexagons on the
desk and ceiling and the
blue circles of the rug, reception introduces the geometry
theme at the W Doha Hotel &
Residences spa
PHOTOGRAPHY Eric Laignel
www.united-designers.com

HBA/HIRSCH BEDNER ASSOCIATES

PROJECT Four Seasons
Resort Seychelles
STANDOUT Five cliff-top
spa pavilions, including
one for yoga, offer a natural
materials palette and the
opportunity to contemplate
sweeping Indian Ocean
views
PHOTOGRAPHY Peter Mealin
www.hbadesign.com

Clockwise from top left: The Finnish-plywood tabletops were made in different shapes to interlock. Tables cascade from steel lintels between the second and third floors of the brick building. Tabletops were coated in black resin and linked with steel or plywood connectors. Where the tables floated above the ground, the maple legs were upturned.

"TABLE CLOTH," LOS ANGELES

Taking center stage at the University of California, Los Angeles, "Table Cloth" explored Benjamin Ball and Gaston Nogues's ongoing interests in space modulation, pop-up architecture, and new uses for standard components. Yet this project went further. For the first time, the partners based a composition on repetitions of just a single object—more specifically a custom table with a top of Finnish plywood, coated in black resin, and three legs of turned maple. Linked with custom devices in steel or plywood, a process that took six staffers 10 days, the tables became a swath that could be draped from existing steel lintels on the brick facade of UCLA's school of music. Tables higher up were upturned, their legs bristling. When the tables reached the ground, they flipped right-side-up and spilled outward. The result was eminently multipurpose. Sometimes it worked as a stage set for performances by a jazz ensemble or a string quartet. During the academic day, lectures took place there—not to mention general hanging out.

Ball-Nogues Studio

WINNER INSTALLATION

PROJECT TEAM BENJAMIN JENETT; JAMES JONES; AYODH KAMATH; JONATHAN KITCHENS; ALISON KUNG; DEBORAH LEHMAN; BRIAN SCHIRK; RACHEL SHILLANDER
PHOTOGRAPHY SCOTT MAYORAL
www.ball-nogues.com

BALL-NOGUES STUDIO

PROJECT "Built to Wear," Hong Kong

STANDOUT Part of the Shenzhen & Hong Kong Bi-City Biennale of Urbanism/ Architecture, this architecturally scaled suspended structure comprised 15,000 pieces of American Apparel clothing

PHOTOGRAPHY Benjamin Ball/ Ball-Nogues Studio

www.ball-nogues.com

GANYMEDE DESIGN GROUP

PROJECT "Schuff-Perini Climber," Phoenix

STANDOUT Found objects dot this three-story steel "dreamscape" at the Children's Museum of Phoenix, encouraging children and adults to climb

PHOTOGRAPHY Timmerman Photography

www.ganymededesign.com

CL3 ARCHITECTS

PROJECT "Route D," Hong Kong

STANDOUT Bamboo poles painted Chinese red composed a free-span bridge and canopy between two buildings

PHOTOGRAPHY Nirut Benjabanbot/CL3 Architects

www.cl3.com

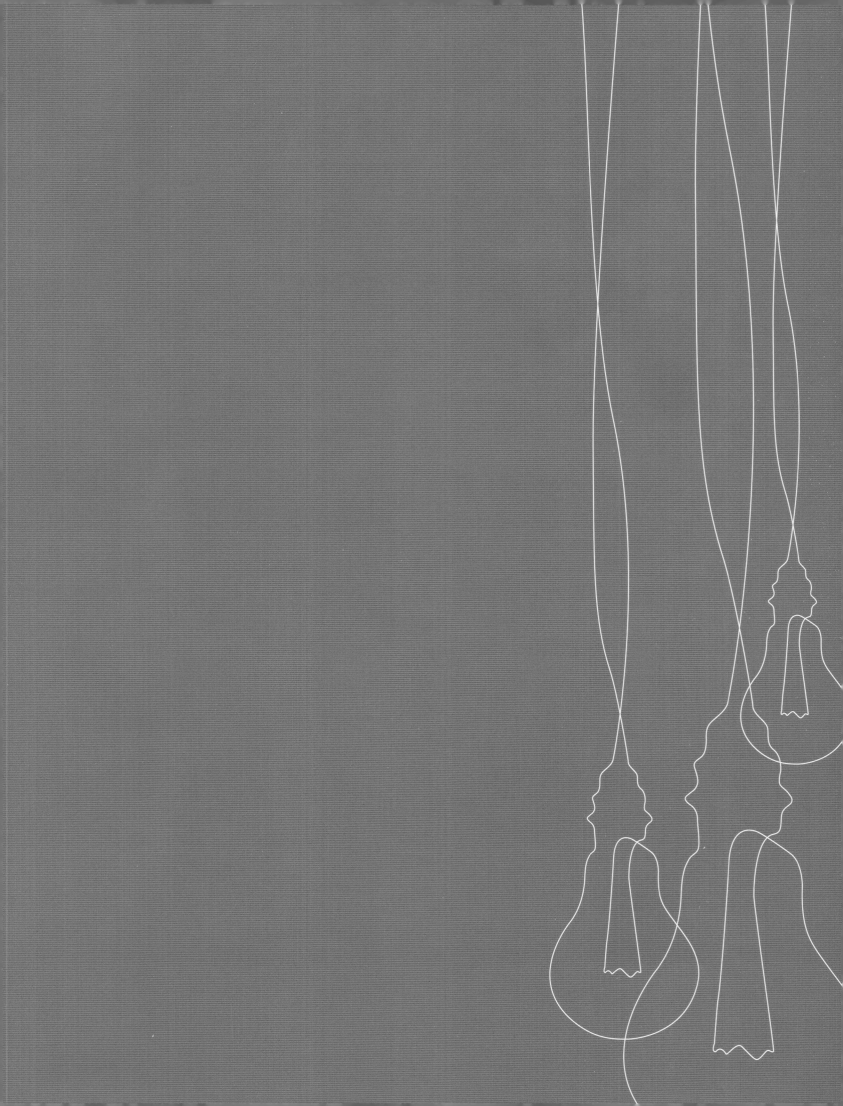

NATIVE CHILD AND FAMILY SERVICES OF TORONTO

Providing social and cultural support for aboriginals, this nonprofit now occupies a 35,000-square-foot downtown building, consolidating four previous offices. Principal Dean Goodman established a visual connection for visitors through natural materials and original art. Meetings and drumming sessions take place in a longhouse-style structure with a honeycomb interior of Eastern white cedar illuminated by pendant fixtures made from bundling used fluorescent tubes. Pendant globes hang in the reception area, where a desk in yellow-birch heartwood is shaped like an eye. The roof terrace is paved with limestone slabs and planted with sweet grass, sage, tobacco, and other species native to the Great Lakes region. In one corner stands a cedar-clad healing lodge. In the center, tree-trunk stools surround a fire circle.

Levitt Goodman
Architects

WINNER INSTITUTIONAL

PROJECT TEAM DANIEL BARTMAN; CHRISTIE PEARSON; LIANA BRESLER;
LEIGH JENEROUX; JASON LEE; LIA MASTON; KRIS PAYNE; TYLER WALKER

PHOTOGRAPHY BEN RAHN/A-FRAME

www.levittgoodmanarchitects.com

Clockwise from far left: The yellow-birch heartwood reception desk is custom. An existing concrete-slab floor was reground and stained with a geometric pattern. The white-cedar "longhouse" is used for ceremonies, meetings, and workshops. Pine log stools form a fire circle near the rooftop sweat lodge. The longhouse is lit by pendants assembled from recycled fluorescent tubes.

1100: ARCHITECT

PROJECT Battery Park City Library, New York

STANDOUT The accent color may be tangerine orange, with chairs by Jens Risom and Verner Panton, but the LEED certification is solid Gold

PHOTOGRAPHY Michael Moran

www.1100architect.com

OLSON KUNDIG ARCHITECTS

PROJECT Whatcom Museum, Bellingham, Washington

STANDOUT A double-glazed wall, arced to follow the sun's path, brings sunlight into the museum's newest branch

PHOTOGRAPHY Benjamin Benschneider

www.olsonkundigarchitects.com

JOHN RONAN ARCHITECTS

PROJECT Christ the King Jesuit College Preparatory School, Chapel of Saint Ignatius Loyola, Chicago

STANDOUT This high school's cladding of fiber-cement panels gives way to glass-block walls at the corner occupied by the chapel

PHOTOGRAPHY Nathan Kirkman

www.jrarch.com

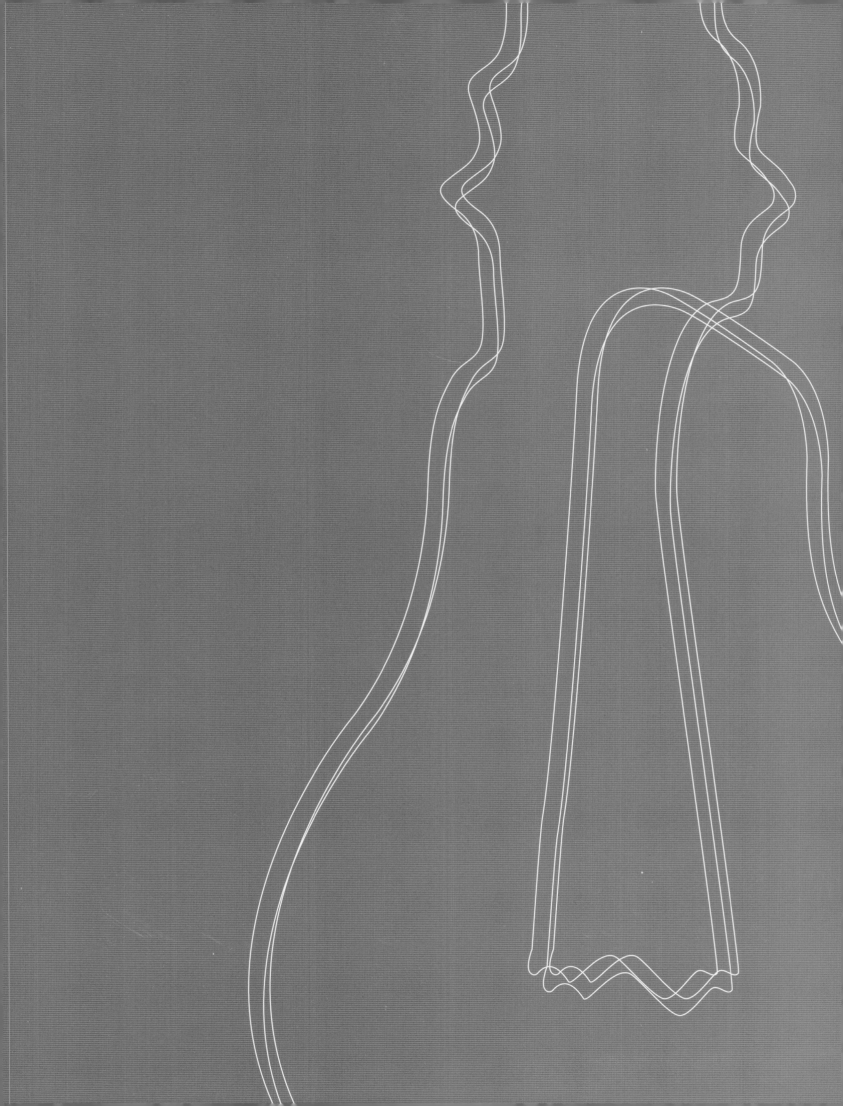

Architecture in Formation

Clockwise from left:
A guest bathroom is compact and efficient. A giant video is projected onto the windowless rear wall of the apartment. The guest bath shower has a built-in bench. The powder room's custom sink and wall-mounted Duravit toilet are anchored by a swath of 4-inch-wide Santos mahogany flooring planks that wrap up the wall. The master bath's shower has Thasos marble flooring and hand-troweled concrete walls. Blu Dot bar stools echo the kitchen's tessellated geometry, inspired by the existing columns.

LOFT, NEW YORK

Banish all thoughts of "man cave" at this bachelor Wall Street trader's sophisticated loft. Inspired by the faceted capitals of the space's existing concrete columns, principal Matthew Bremer used 3-D and parametric modeling to design angled planes in white-painted plasterboard, then lit them with a mix of fluorescent, halogen, and incandescent fixtures. Occupying the center of the narrow, 3,000-square-foot plan is the kitchen, where bar stools with faceted steel seats, powder-coated a slightly creamier white than the walls, pull up to an island with a counter cantilevering over the mahogany floor. The same mahogany flows into the living area at one end of the kitchen and the den at the other. In the powder room, the planks also sneak up the wall that anchors a toilet by Sieger Design and a similarly boxy Thassos marble sink. More marble combines with limestone, glacier-white Corian, and concrete in the master bathroom. Bremer calls it a "futuristic luxury aircraft."

PROJECT TEAM PAULO FLORES; RICARDO KENDALL; VICTOR ORTEGA

PHOTOGRAPHY TOM POWEL

www.architecture-if.com

MIDTOWN PENTHOUSE, NEW YORK

Workshop/APD

HONOREE KITCHEN & BATH

When Workshop/APD's client learned that the duplex penthouse and roof of a 12-story Manhattan building were on the market, he sprang at the chance to move on up. Then he hired principals Matthew Berman and Andrew Kotchen to convert the 2,700-square-foot industrial loft into a sun-splashed haven replete with exquisite natural finishes and crisp architectural detailing.

A media room and two bedrooms now occupy what was once a very compartmentalized apartment on the building's top floor. The master suite is appropriately grand, with a dressing area and spalike bathroom. Warming up the firm's signature minimalism are earthy, masculine materials—wide-plank flooring, a charcoal quartz-composite vanity, koto-veneer casework, and split-faced quartzite wall tile—not to mention a gas and steel hearth. Lightening the mood, a claw-foot tub sprayed with metallic midnight-blue auto paint rests on a platform alternating teak strips with black rubber gaskets. Where the teak continues into the adjacent acid-etched glass-box shower, the architects simply skipped the gaskets so water can drain through.

Patinated stainless steel was used for the Donald Judd–inspired shelving, shower-control pylon, and atrium staircase ascending to the roof-level kitchen and living zone. Up in this aerie, a wall of faceted glass windows overlook the Empire State Building and lushly landscaped private decks—complete with perfect emerald grass and a modernist pergola.

Clockwise from top left: A feature wall of quartzite tile defines the penthouse's master bathroom. Open shelving of patinated stainless steel incorporates a towel bar. The apartment's upper level leads to a private garden that wraps around the roof's water tower. ⬎

Clockwise from far left: The datum line of the bathroom cabinetry extends to the feature wall, forming a hearth. A floating staircase sculpted from patinated stainless steel ascends to the kitchen and living level. Stainless steel was also used in the kitchen. Acid-etched glass panels bracket the claw-foot tub, which sits on a teak platform.

PROJECT TEAM ANDREW HART; ZACHARY HELMERS

PHOTOGRAPHY TOM OLCOTT

www.workshopapd.com

Clockwise from left:
*Sand used the same
Indian rosewood
veneer throughout the
apartment, including
wall panels in the
master bath. A full-
height glass wall
separates the guest
quarter's blue-marble
wet zone from the
sleep area. Orange
marble distinguishes
the powder room.
Rosewood also
surfaces the kitchen
cabinetry and marble-
topped bar face;
stools are by E15.*

MEHTA RESIDENCE, MIAMI BEACH

This waterfront Miami Beach condominium boasted 3,000 square feet plus a killer view of the ocean through big picture windows. What it lacked, though, was a contemporary layout geared to entertaining. Enter principal Larissa Sand, who swooped in and transformed the apartment to echo the broad sweep of beach outside.

Sand reworked the public areas into a free-flowing volume, positioning the intimate quarters behind glass partitions fitted with shades—to be pulled only when privacy is needed. Concrete structural shear walls uncovered during the gut renovation were left exposed, contrasting with refined wood and marble finishes. The living areas center around a minimalist open kitchen featuring Indian rosewood—veneered cabinetry with carefully book-matched horizontal graining. The same wood was used in the rest of the apartment, too, defining portals and closet doors meticulously detailed to appear as continuous floor-to-ceiling paneling.

The decor of the bathrooms reiterates this sense of openness and tactility. A glass wall separates the guest suite's sleeping quarters and wet area, clad in a richly variegated blue marble keyed to the sky and sea. The intense orange marble in the powder room reflects the heritage of the designer's Indian-born client, for whom Sand suggested a palette of saturated colors. Striking a more neutral note, flooring throughout is beach-approved brushed limestone—evocative of an endless stretch of sand.

HONOREE **KITCHEN & BATH**

Sand Studios

PROJECT TEAM BEN DAMRON; TRAVIS HAYES; MARCUS WILLIS
PHOTOGRAPHY KEN HAYDEN
www.sandstudios.com

OSMOSE DESIGN

PROJECT Finley residence, Portland, Oregon

STANDOUT A couple's interest in art and design informs the master bathroom's hand-painted mural, the kitchen's canted island treatment and large-scale canvas, and the master bedroom's shoe storage

PHOTOGRAPHY Lincoln Barbour

www.osmosedesign.com

Clockwise from top left: The 10-story atrium's cantilevered meeting pods were inspired by shipping containers. The 26 pods are marked by vinyl graphics with crosshatch lines referring to the steel grid on the building's exterior. Ottomans by Toshiyuki Kita furnish a meeting space. Vinyl graphics enliven the built-in Corian work surface in a dining lounge. Behind the Corian reception desk, signage is composed of stainless-steel tubes, some partially wrapped in vinyl.

MACQUARIE GROUP, SYDNEY, AUSTRALIA

"Australians are feisty. They're a different breed," Clive Wilkinson says. So is he: an *Interior Design* Hall of Fame member born in South Africa and based in Los Angeles, with multiple high-octane ad agencies in his portfolio. At Macquarie, his debut in the financial-services arena, he was asked to provide not buttoned-up bankers' offices or a bull-pen trading floor but the model known as activity-based working. Unlike "hoteling," that means there's a place for everyone, just not a fixed place. Wilkinson had to get people traveling through the 330,000-square-foot building both horizontally and vertically. To that end, a monumental stair rises through the 10 levels of the central atrium. Jutting into it on every level are an assortment of meeting pods, their boxy forms a reference to the shipping containers of Sydney Harbour, just blocks away. Wilkinson's boxes, how-ever, are fronted in clear glass. Call it design's contribution to transparency in banking.

WINNER **OFFICE / LARGE**

Clive Wilkinson Architects

PROJECT TEAM JOHN MEACHEM; ALEXIS RAPPAPORT; RUBEN SMUDDE; NEIL MUNTZEL
PHOTOGRAPHY SHANNON McGRATH
www.clivewilkinson.com

Pollack Architecture

HONOREE OFFICE / LARGE

APX ALARM, PROVO, UTAH

APX Alarm employs 3,500 students annually to fan across America selling some 150,000 security systems. Back at the company's Provo, Utah, headquarters, 850 additional employees organize that herculean outreach effort and oversee customer service and technical support.

Pollack Architecture principal David Galullo assembled the 125,000-square-foot interiors, establishing openness and transparency while making ample use of wallet-friendly treatments like photo murals and carpet tile—in 27 patterns—to keep the budget to $45 per square foot. The double-height reception, with its glass feature wall

and blond-wood accents, advances the airy tone. Glass also fronts both sides of the 90-foot-long concrete-floored corridors, or "main streets," where conference- and meeting-room entrances are marked with angled canopies. Vinyl block letters spell out customer comments on the glazed walls enclosing a pair of private dining rooms, furnished with reclaimed-wood tables. For group bonding, there's a 15,000-square-foot café, populated with bent-plywood armchairs, as well as more intimate "huddle" rooms featuring lounge chairs by Ron Arad and Charles and Ray Eames.

Bench-style workstations have customized storage but no partitions, to keep views of the nearby Cascade Mountains unobstructed. In the open-plan environment, zones are demarcated via color-coded wall paint. Work areas are either orange-yellow or chartreuse, executive offices are steel blue, and oxblood draws the eye to a rustic lounge—dubbed the "lodge"—where a mounted elk head shows off the CEO's best shot to date.

Clockwise from top left: The reception area features a maple-veneer and plastic-laminate desk. The words of satisfied APX Alarm customers are spelled out in vinyl on the glass wall of a "huddle" room featuring Ron Arad's Tom Vac chairs. A photomural by George Marks covers a wall in a meeting room. Another meeting room showcases a David Sherman photomural.

PROJECT TEAM JOELLE ROSANDER; NATHANIEL HAYNES; TUAN LOUV

PHOTOGRAPHY ERIC LAIGNEL

www.pollackarch.com

Clockwise from left:
Bertjan Pot's playful
Random Light
pendants illuminate
the café. A photomural
by Robert W. Madden
takes over one wall
of the sales support
center. A mounted elk
head keeps watch
over the café's lodge-
theme lounge.

GENSLER

PROJECT Trading firm, Chicago
STANDOUT A café and lounge with furnishings by Piero Lissoni and
Achille and Pier Giacomo Castiglioni help to attract top talent
PHOTOGRAPHY Christopher Barrett
www.gensler.com

GENSLER

PROJECT Panduit, Tinley Park, Illinois
STANDOUT Slim furniture and a spare materials palette of
glass, granite, and reclaimed redwood convey the efficiency
of a cutting-edge technology developer
PHOTOGRAPHY Christopher Barrett
www.gensler.com

PRODUCTION COMPANY, LOS ANGELES

Friends since SCI-Arc, Joey Shimoda and Andy Waisler finally got a chance to collaborate—on a project for a third pal, a super-creative in the entertainment business. He commissioned the architects to join a pair of industrial buildings to form, essentially, a miniature movie studio. Concrete flooring and reclaimed-oak ceiling fins give continuity to the 16,000-square-foot interior. Taking cues from cinematic techniques, Shimoda and Waisler established a series of striking long views and detailed close-ups. The money shot comes right at the entry, where you catch a glimpse of the reception lounge by peering between a freestanding unit's walnut shelves stocked with robot toys and furniture miniatures. Mystery and transparency draw you inside, where the layout is anything but linear. Three staircases and an elevator offer passage upstairs, where executive offices owe their double height to the new glass box on top. The adjacent roof deck is an alfresco lounge, complete with a putting green.

Shimoda Design Group and Andy Waisler

WINNER OFFICE / MIDSIZE

PROJECT TEAM DAN ALLEN; TODD TUNTLAND; DAVID KHUONG;
SUE CHANG; LUCI IWASAKI; ANDRE KRAUSE; MCKENNA COLE
PHOTOGRAPHY BENNY CHAN/FOTOWORKS
www.shimodadesign.com

Clockwise from far left: Anchored in the reception's polished concrete floor, anodized-aluminum posts support walnut shelving. The founder's office overhangs the reception area, where reclaimed oak beams were added to the ceiling. Seismic concerns required adding a steel beam for structural bracing in the founder's office. Access to the roof deck is via a galvanized-steel stairway or an ipe-clad elevator tower.

NERI & HU DESIGN AND RESEARCH OFFICE

PROJECT Neri & Hu Design and Research Office and Design Republic, Shanghai, China

STANDOUT An architecture firm and a design retailer, both run by the same husband and wife, share office space in a three-story black-stained concrete box above a teak-clad storefront

PHOTOGRAPHY Derryck Menere

www.nhdro.com

GENSLER

PROJECT Hyundai Capital America, Irvine, California

STANDOUT If chairs by Verner Panton, Eero Saarinen, and Eero Aarnio aren't sufficient, an oak staircase doubles as bleacher seating for seminars and screenings

PHOTOGRAPHY Ryan Gobuty/Gensler

www.gensler.com

OWP/P CANNON DESIGN

PROJECT Trading firm, Chicago

STANDOUT An energetic corporate culture comes through in the dynamic angles and vivid colors, particularly the chartreuse that shows up everywhere from feature walls to the lounge's Konstantin Grcic chairs

PHOTOGRAPHY Christopher Barrett

www.owpp.com

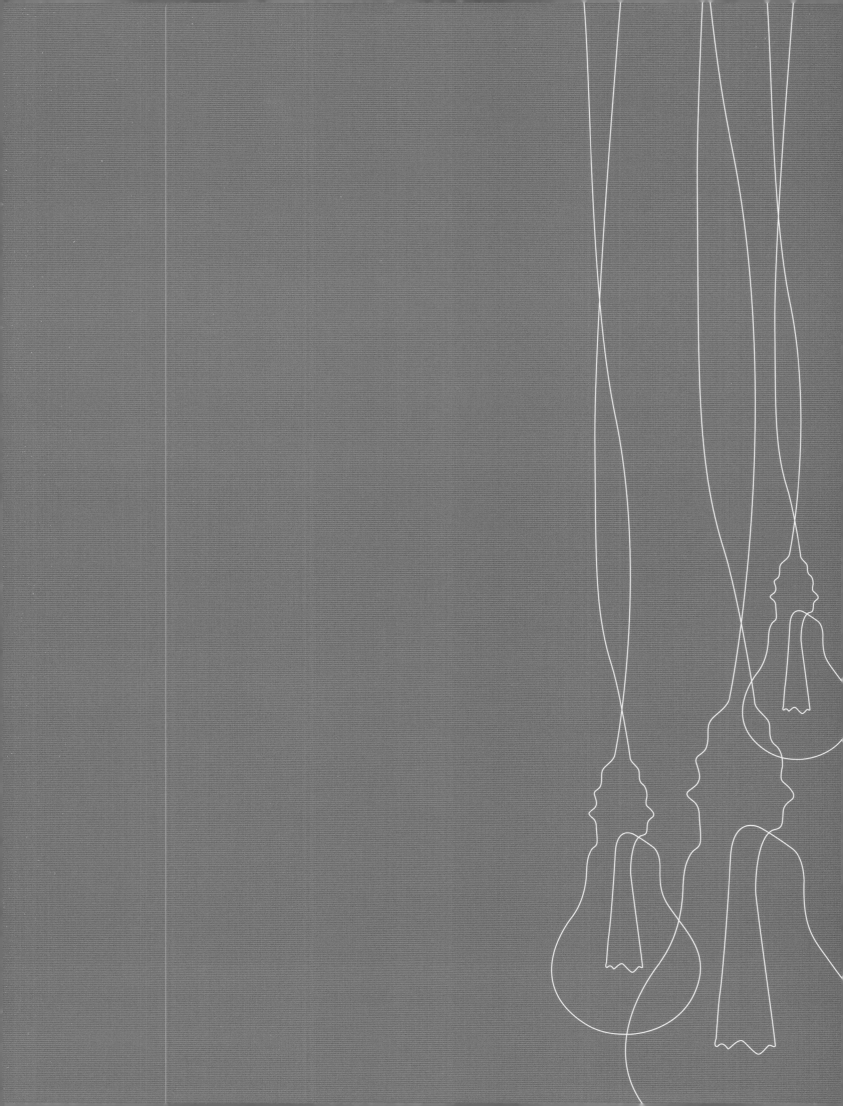

Asked to transform raw space in an office park into the headquarters of the U.S. Data Corporation, a supplier of marketing information such as mailing lists, Randy Brown revisited a concept he'd developed long ago for the company's previous location, downtown. The angled walls once found in the former space now wrap onto the ceiling in the new one—jagged forms realized in no-frills gypsum-board painted an electric lime green inspired by the flashing cursor of an ancient computer monitor that Brown unearthed in the server room. He extended sight lines through the 5,000-square-foot interior by punching large apertures through the green planes along the main circulation spine, which begins at reception and ends at open workstations. A few other walls are clad in siding typically used for agricultural sheds: corrugated galvanized-steel panels that are ubiquitous in rural Nebraska. And the front wall of the conference room is glass displaying large and small black numbers, the area codes and zip codes that U.S. Data targets in the Midwest and California.

Randy Brown Architects

WINNER **OFFICE** / **SMALL**

Clockwise from far left: Fluorescent tubes backlight the conference room's custom ceiling fixture of frosted acrylic and painted steel. Le Corbusier's LC2 chair anchors the main corridor. On the conference room's glass front, satin-vinyl film lists area codes and zip codes targeted by the company. A custom door of maple plywood pivots open to an office sided in galvanized steel.

PROJECT TEAM BRIAN KELLY; ANDREA KELLY; NEIL LEGBAND

PHOTOGRAPHY FARSHID ASSASSI

www.randybrownarchitects.com

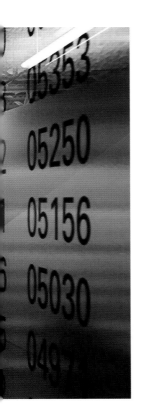

Flooring is sealed concrete; the cursor on a green-screen computer monitor inspired the color of the wall paint.

MINISTRY OF DESIGN

PROJECT Face to Face, Singapore
STANDOUT Light-dark contrasts define this office building's facade as well as interior elements including a spiral staircase from the ground level to basement meeting rooms
PHOTOGRAPHY Edward Hendricks/CI&A Photography
www.modonline.com

AXELROD DESIGN

PROJECT Cargal Group, Lod, Israel
STANDOUT Inside a factory that makes cardboard packaging, a slot window in a concrete-block box offers a glimpse of corporate offices and meeting rooms
PHOTOGRAPHY Amit Geron
www.axelrodarchitects.com

MERZPROJECT

PROJECT Merzproject, Phoenix
STANDOUT Before merging with Shepley Bulfinch, an *Interior Design* Giant, this small studio renovated a 1950's building and moved into the top floor
PHOTOGRAPHY Matt Winquist
www.shepleybulfinch.com

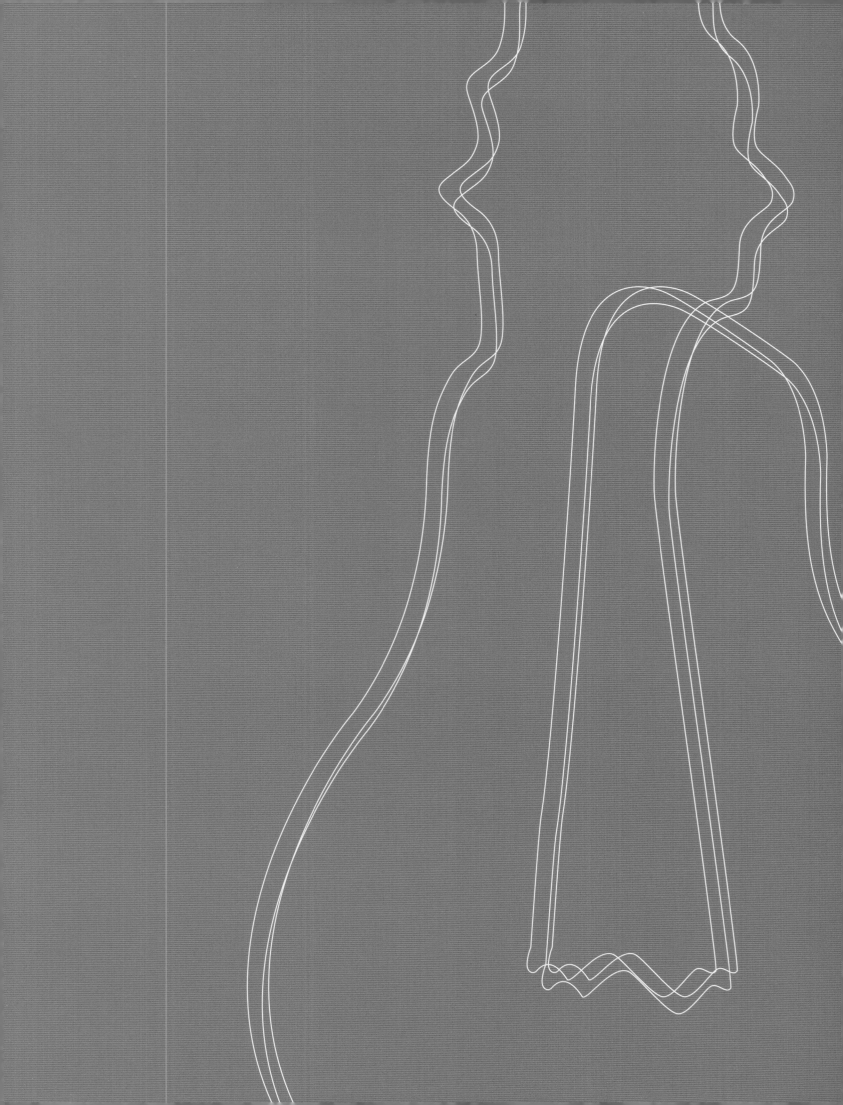

Studios
Architecture

WINNER OFFICE RENOVATION

GREY GROUP, NEW YORK

Clockwise from left: The double-height "town hall" presentation room features birch stacking chairs and MDF panels machined with an argyle pattern developed by Pentagram. In the open workspace, reclaimed wood sheathes a storage and seating unit. The office is visible from Fifth Avenue through the building's arched limestone entrance. The courtyard centers on a potted bamboo plant. Restroom signage was painted to appear projected.

Headquartered in the same modernist tower since the "Mad Men" era, the marketing and communications firm formerly known as Grey Advertising has moved to a limestone landmark. Studios principal Tom Krizmanic kept the shock to a minimum by seamlessly integrating a sequence of contemporary spaces into the 100-year-old architecture. Because the arched entrance is glazed, even casual passersby can see straight through the lobby and into the garden atrium that serves as a vertical hub. It's surrounded by workstations for account executives, studios for creatives, print and audio-video production suites, and a town hall with a wall that slides away to fit 325 people for bimonthly meetings. Krizmanic used wood reclaimed from Pennsylvania barns for reception desks, break-out areas, meeting-room enclosures, and a movable screen setting off a state-of-the-art presentation center; workstations, meanwhile, have bamboo tops. Eco-friendliness and continuity meet with the mid-century furnishings, brought over from the agency's previous location.

PROJECT TEAM TODD DeGARMO; BRENT CAPRON; GEOFF DEOLD; WESLEY WONG; JANE RICHTER; SARA WHITE

PHOTOGRAPHY NIKOLAS KOENIG (1-4); PETER MAUSS/ESTO (5)

www.studiosarchitecture.com

STUDIOS ARCHITECTURE

PROJECT Orrick, Herrington & Sutcliffe, New York

STANDOUT This law firm's maverick character comes through in the formed-birch slats that allow glimpses into the boardroom, located right above a café featuring an LED chandelier with crystal pendants

PHOTOGRAPHY Eric Laignel

www.studiosarchitecture.com

GENSLER

PROJECT Ogilvy & Mather, New York

STANDOUT A 1913 chocolate factory, now certified LEED Gold, houses a marketing and communications firm where interconnectivity takes the form of open libraries and conference rooms with sliding walls

PHOTOGRAPHY Chris Leonard/ Gensler

www.gensler.com

STUDIOS ARCHITECTURE

PROJECT Guess, Los Angeles

STANDOUT At a warehouse once owned by Howard Hughes, stamped vinyl repurposed from handbags became the multipurpose room's seating pads, and an ad campaign yielded the lounge's Claudia Schiffer silk screen

PHOTOGRAPHY Benny Chan/Fotoworks

www.studiosarchitecture.com

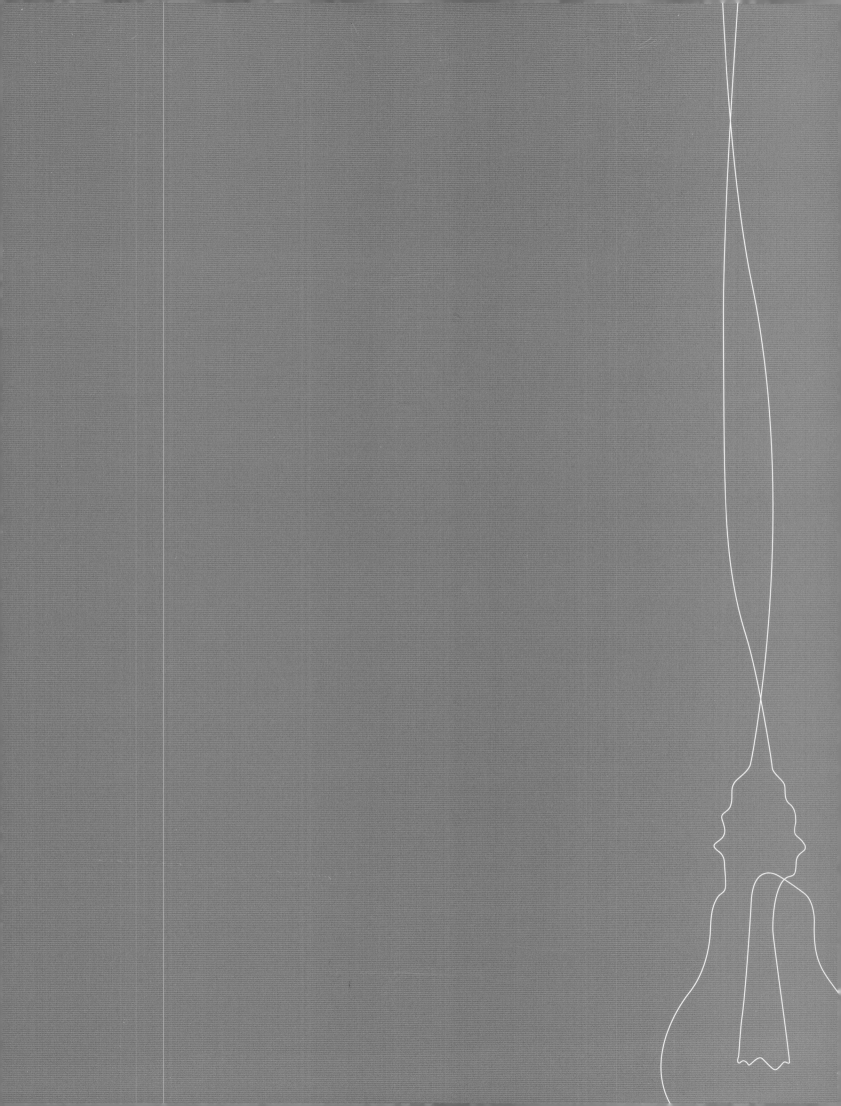

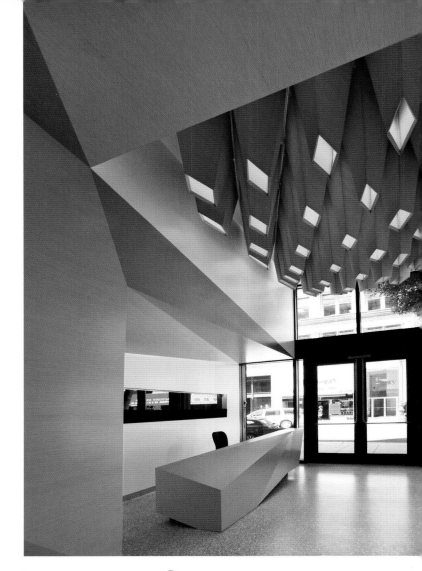

1 KEARNY STREET, SAN FRANCISCO

A 1902 building, its 1964 annex by Charles Moore, and a new high-rise by the Office of Charles F. Bloszies, AIA, have combined to form a complex not far from the galleries and museums of the Yerba Buena arts district. To satisfy the city's percent-for-art requirement for commercial developments, Lisa Iwamoto and Craig Scott were hired to create a site-specific installation for the 860-square-foot shared lobby, and the result is *Lightfold*. They blurred the line between art and design by drawing inspiration from the ornamental surfaces found in century-old architecture, specifically the ceiling coffers. Above the reception desk, the imaginary coffers are scaled up and extruded in sustainable maple veneer to produce an abstracted chandelier fitted with LEDs programmed to dim and brighten according to ambient conditions. Maple veneer also surfaces angular wall and ceiling planes along the corridor that leads back to the elevators.

IwamotoScott Architecture

WINNER PUBLIC SPACE

PROJECT TEAM RYAN GOLENBERG; CHRISTINA KANEVA; ALAN LU; BLAKE ALTSHULER; DAVID SWAIN

PHOTOGRAPHY CRAIG SCOTT/IWAMOTOSCOTT

www.iwamotoscott.com

Clockwise from far left: Comprising dimmable LEDs, the angular chandelier illuminates reception just inside the lobby entrance. Diffusors are made of folded maple veneer. Visible through a clerestory, the installation contributes to curb-side appeal. One-way mirrors veil a video display wall.

NORR

HONOREE PUBLIC SPACE

ALLSTREAM CENTRE, TORONTO

__Clockwise from top left:__ A feature wall comprising three different varieties of limestone forms a focal point in the double-height atrium. The lobby has been restored to its historic 1929 design. Newly added plywood portals in the second-floor circulation gallery draw attention to conference room entrances. The architect removed columns in the ballroom—which seats 3,000—to create a 150-foot-long expanse of space.

Toronto's Exhibition Place encompasses nearly 200 lakefront acres dotted with pavilions that host an impressive 4.5 million visitors a year. One icon on the property, the 1929 Automotive Building, started out as an elegant showcase for the latest roadsters. More recently, NORR remodeled the 196,000-square-foot landmark into a conference facility, newly christened the Allstream Centre.

The conversion restored the original masonry facade to its period glamour. Lobbies, too, are shipshape again, with Depression-era checkerboard floors, modern plasterwork, and wrought-iron railings all refreshed. Principal David Clusiau saw the project as a chance to look forward as well as back, and he accomplished the former goal via ecofriendly enhancements. Rainwater is now recycled for flushing sanitary facilities. High-performance replica windows reduce the transfer of heat and save energy. Low-emitting materials were used throughout. And instead of cluttering up landfill, three quarters of construction waste was repurposed.

Other new features include a 44,000-square-foot column-free ballroom—divisible into two acoustically separate rooms with high-tech AV capabilities—plus a series of second-floor conference rooms. The latter are pulled back from the exterior wall, creating a sunny circulation gallery offering lake views. Perhaps the most spectacular statement, though, is the atrium's double-height feature wall with a Mondrianesque collage of limestone blocks.

PROJECT TEAM EMON LOU; IRENE JACKIW;
AGA KACPRZAK; DAVID SPRY
PHOTOGRAPHY SHAI GIL
www.norr.com

Slade Architecture

HONOREE PUBLIC SPACE

184 KENT AVENUE, BROOKLYN, NEW YORK

Best known as the architect of the U.S. Supreme Court and New York's iconic Woolworth Building, Cass Gilbert also designed humbler structures, including a waterfront warehouse in the Williamsburg section of Brooklyn. Originally built for the Austin, Nichols & Company Warehouse—which own Wild Turkey—and later used as a grocery warehouse, the 500,000-square-foot building has now been reborn as funky loft rentals, courtesy of Slade Architecture.

Principals Hayes and James Slade oversaw every aspect of the interior conversion, from apartment floor plans to amenities, such as a multipurpose lounge, gym, and children's playroom. The Slades' design is sensitive to the 1915 shell while updating it for a contemporary—and decidedly hip—clientele. Rather than map out identical floor plans for the 400 lofts, layouts cleverly sidestep structural eccentricities. In the public areas, a nature-themed decor nods to the new waterfront park taking shape outside. The reception zone is capped by a teak canopy perforated to evoke sun-dappled trees. Suggesting a lush lawn, bright green goat-hair broadloom and matching area rugs define functions in the loftlike open lounge, enlivened with temporary wall installations organized by the Brooklyn Arts Council. Walnut paneling demarcates the library, while earth-tone wallpapers define areas devoted to pastimes like Ping-Pong, billiards, and Wii—not to mention the appreciation of historic architecture.

Clockwise from left:
The lobby occupies the space of a former loading dock. A drop ceiling above the reception area is CNC-milled teak, the same material that surfaces the desk and the columns. Sculptural seating like Hella Jongerius's button-tufted Polder sofa defines activity zones in the open-plan lounge. The lobby was designed to accommodate such communal activities as Ping-Pong and billiards.

PROJECT TEAM EMILY ANDERSEN; TIAN GAO; CHIA-PING LIN; JEFF WANDERSMAN; STEPHANIE WONG; PALMER THOMPSON-MOSS
PHOTOGRAPHY TIAN GAO/SLADE ARCHITECTURE
www.sladearch.com

ONE PLUS PARTNERSHIP

PROJECT Broadway Cinemas,
Kunming, China
STANDOUT Metal-capped wooden rods,
protruding from the wall behind the ticket
counter, spell out the name of the mul-
tiplex, while cylinders of mirror-polished
stainless steel descend from the ceiling
PHOTOGRAPHY Ajax Law Ling Kit and
Virginia Lung/One Plus Partnership
www.onepluspartnership.com

Shelton, Mindel & Associates

WINNER APARTMENT

SOHO PENTHOUSE, NEW YORK

Creating a duplex penthouse from 2,500 square feet of raw space at a building by Ateliers Jean Nouvel, *Interior Design* Hall of Fame members Peter Shelton and Lee Mindel decided that the stunning curtain wall, with its large-scale aluminum frame, would inform their work inside. Thus, a two-story stack of interlocking volumes pulls away from the windows, leaving them in plain view. Hugging the double-height perimeter that results from this major move are living and dining areas furnished courtesy of Poul Henningsen, Poul Kjaerholm, Arne Jacobsen, Ludwig Mies van der Rohe, and Jean Prouvé. Meanwhile, the volumes' white-lacquered surfaces and walnut paneling conceal the study, guest suite, and powder room. Shelton and Mindel tucked the open kitchen beneath an overhang formed by the upstairs master suite. Because its ceiling is glass, the designers provided some shade and intimacy by suspending a panel of painted MDF overhead. This bright yellow rectangle also plays a more cerebral role, recalling the spatial explorations of Gerrit Rietveld and Theo Van Doesburg.

Clockwise from left:
The bold yellow of the canopy below the skylight nods to De Stijl. The living room features a Mies van der Rohe daybed alongside custom sofas and coffee tables by Shelton Mindel & Associates. An Antony Gormley ball-bearing sculpture enlivens the dining area, furnished with a Poul Henningsen Artichoke pendant and Arne Jacobsen chairs. The guest bedroom wall is covered in a custom upholstery by Dune.

PROJECT TEAM MICHAEL NEAL; IVAN ZIDAROV;
GRACE SIERRA; LINDSAY DIETZ

PHOTOGRAPHY MICHAEL MORAN

www.sheltonmindel.com

Clockwise from left: The view from the apartment takes in the Santa Monica bay; the settee is upholstered in burlap. Walz used milk paint on most of the walls. A bench from Sri Lanka faces the living area's steel-plate fireplace and, displayed above it, David Hockney's pigmented Paper Pool and an array of Gorelik's bronzes. ➤

Walzworkinc

HONOREE APARTMENT

GORELIK RESIDENCE, LOS ANGELES

California artist Richard Diebenkorn painted his celebrated Ocean Park series just blocks from the 1,000-square-foot apartment of retired investor Guy Gorelik and his wife, Joyce, a watercolorist and sculptor. Not coincidentally, their interior designer, Kevin Walz, is a trained painter, too, which explains the walls awash in lustrous shades of ocean blue, mustard, and fern. Top coats of oyster white or gray-blue—sanded and then waxed—imbue them with the subtlety of Roman frescoes.

Indeed, the *Interior Design* Hall of Famer, who splits his time between New York and Rome, imported a dose of Italian luxury. Puglian limestone delivers durability for the kitchen counter as well as the bathroom sinks and flooring. A Sardinian cooperative provided the bedroom's handwoven wall-to-wall carpet in unpigmented wool. Throughout, rich wood finishes play off the polychrome walls: zebrawood panels in the dining area, cedar wardrobes in the bedroom, floor-to-ceiling teak medicine cabinets in the bathroom. The designer teamed with his brother, Barry, to build slender shelves throughout in walnut and carbon fiber, a structure patented for its incredible strength.

A different wood product, cork, plays a starring role in the decor, from the kitchen floor to the custom bed and living room chairs of Walz's own design. But it is another talent's work that truly establishes the sense of home: Art by Joyce Gorelik decorates almost every room.

"The strong colors were what Diebenkorn might've used. It was risky; I wasn't sure it would work"

In the living area, cork chairs by Walz flank a custom tray table by sculptor Erik Anderson. ➤

1 ENTRY

2 STUDY

3 KITCHEN

4 DINING AREA

5 LIVING AREA

6 BEDROOM

0   5   10   20

Clockwise from left:
*Guy Gorelik, an ink
drawing by Oswaldo
Guayasamin,
overlooks the
custom cork bed. A
refurbished Eames
chair sits in a corner
of the bedroom, near
Gorelik watercolors
and wall-mounted
shelving patented by
Walz and his brother,
Barry. A 5-foot-long
slab of Italian
limestone forms the
master bath's double-
trough sink; frosted
glass partially
obscures the shower.
In the study, Gorelik's
The Crying Flag sits
on the custom desk's
inch-thick cork top;
the sofa bed is
upholstered in a
polyester-cotton
blend.*

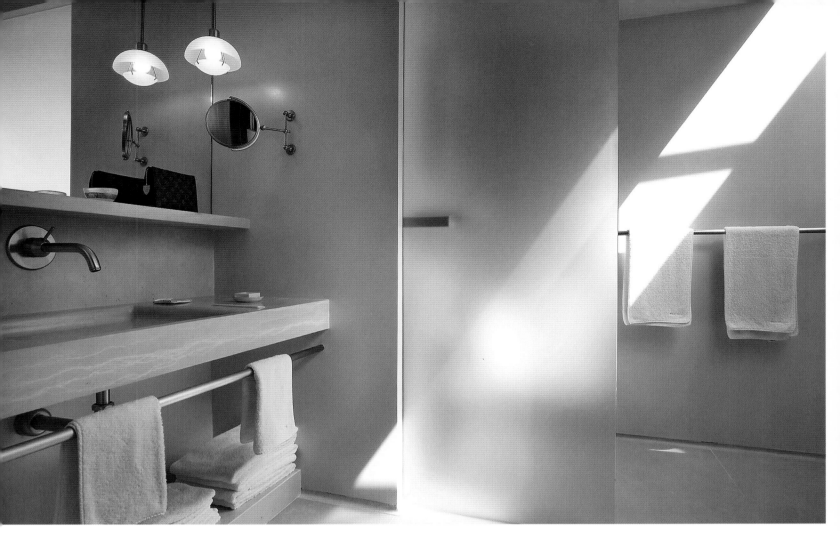

PROJECT TEAM DANIELE CALISI; ROSA TOPPUTO
PHOTOGRAPHY ERIC LAIGNEL
www.walzworkinc.com

ARCHITECTURE IN FORMATION

PROJECT Loft, New York
STANDOUT The angularity of original concrete columns and new plasterboard walls, all painted a brilliant white, contrasts with the mellow mahogany floorboards of this bachelor pad
PHOTOGRAPHY Tom Powel
www.architecture-if.com

D'AQUINO MONACO

PROJECT Apartment, New York
STANDOUT Eliminating prewar-style service corridors and crown moldings, a renovation made way for Italian and French 20th-century furnishings and international contemporary art
PHOTOGRAPHY Peter Murdock
www.daquinomonaco.com

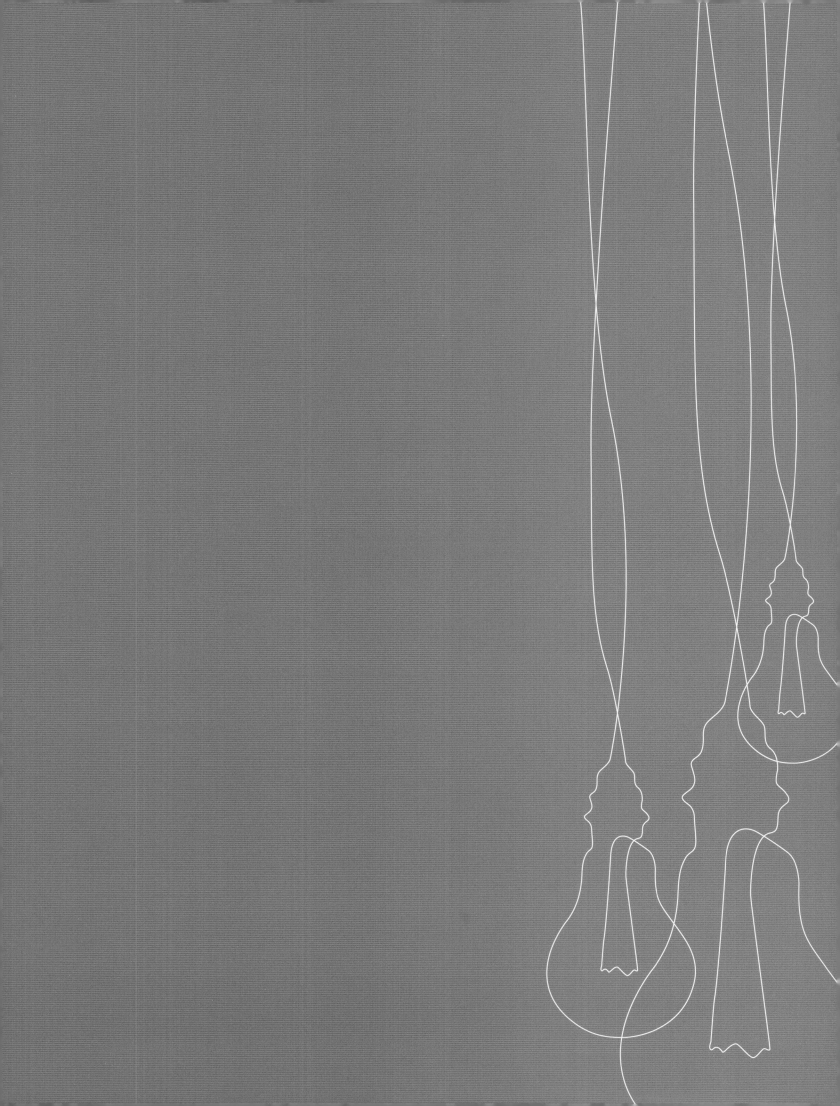

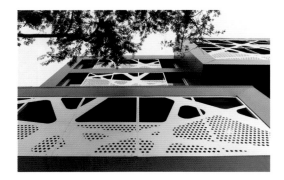

SIERRA BONITA APARTMENTS, LOS ANGELES

Patrick Tighe made certain that this five-story, 50,000-square-foot building looked nothing like an affordable-housing project. He established a lively exterior rhythm by having some units protrude as others recede, and glass this expansive is furthermore rare in affordable housing. Since the street out front is high-traffic Santa Monica Boulevard, the glass needed a scrim of sorts. He responded with laser-cut aluminum abstractions that are mostly metal up to the 3-foot mark and mostly open above, allowing them to double as balustrades. Contrasting with the bold front and rear facades, the central courtyard is a secret garden lush with low-maintenance grasses. The courtyard is surrounded on three sides by the balcony corridors that connect the 42 one-bedroom units, which all manage to squeeze the essentials, plus a walk-in closet, into 620 square feet. On the roof, photovoltaic panels provide enough electricity to power light fixtures in public spaces downstairs. Other solar panels combine with PVC pipe to heat the building's water. Talk about bright ideas.

Tighe Architecture

WINNER **APARTMENT BUILDING**

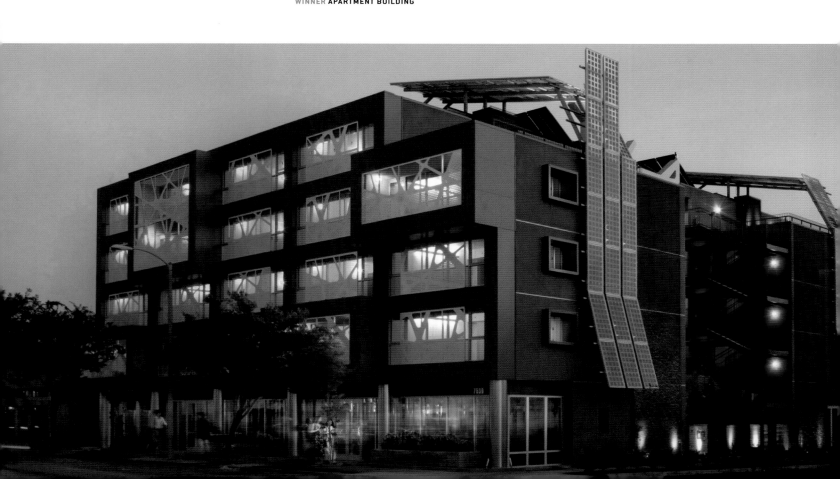

Clockwise from far left: Laser-cut aluminum partially screens the front facade. Bamboo grows in Cor-Ten steel containers in the center courtyard. A custom aluminum clock is mounted on the courtyard's stucco elevator tower, while custom polycarbonate light tubes are bolted to each level's steel floor plate. Windows and doors are aluminum-framed. The building contains 42 residential units, all 620-square-foot one-bedrooms.

PROJECT TEAM YOSUKE HOSHINA; RISA TSUTSUMI; LISA LITTLE; KARLA MUELLER; JAROD POENISCH; MIKE NESBIT; PETE STORY; NICK HOPSON; PHILIP RAMERIZ; EMMY MURATA

PHOTOGRAPHY ART GRAY

www.tighearchitecture.com

ESKEW + DUMEZ + RIPPLE

PROJECT 930 Poydras, New Orleans
STANDOUT The French Quarter's sociable courtyards inspired the idea of grouping all tenant amenities, such as the sky lobby and pool deck, on the same floor of this tower
PHOTOGRAPHY Timothy Hursley
www.eskewdumezripple.com

S. RUSSELL GROVES

PROJECT Lucida, New York
STANDOUT Aiming to introduce LEED Silver–certified luxury to a scruffy corner, the lobby features upholstered seating beneath a polished-nickel chandelier, while the fifth floor offers a game room and a cedar-lined sauna
PHOTOGRAPHY Brad Stein
www.srussellgroves.com

TSAO & McKOWN ARCHITECTS

PROJECT William Beaver House, New York
STANDOUT Glazed yellow bricks punctuate the upper facade, culminating at a penthouse lounge conceived with hotelier André Balazs, one of the developers
PHOTOGRAPHY Richard Bryant/Arcaid
www.tsaomckown.com

The Leader in Opening Glass Walls

NanaWall SL82 Structurally Glazed,
Thermally Broken Aluminum Framed Folding System

The NanaWall SL82 is the winner of 6 design awards:
- Interior Design Best of Year 2010
- Red Dot Product Design Award 2010
- iF Product Design Award 2010
- NeoCon New Product Innovation Merit Award 2010
- Glass Magazine Crystal Achievement Award 2010
- Architectural Record Top Ten Products 2010

Shelter. Transformation. Exhilaration.

Superior engineering and design flexibility ensures unsurpassed durability in all-weather environments while maintaining exceptional performance for years to come.

Showrooms Nationwide   888 868 6643   **nanawall.com**

NanaWall ®
Grand Transformations

RESIDENCE, KONA, HAWAII

Belzberg Architects and MLK Studio

WINNER RESORT HOUSE

Commissioned to build a family vacation compound in the traditional enclave of Hualalai, on the lava-rich western coast of Hawaii's Big Island, Hagy Belzberg went against the grain with a stridently contemporary scheme. The design's bold forms, slide-away glass walls, and numerous water features nonetheless forge a strong connection to the lush island setting.

The 1-acre property comprises five structures, including a screening room and separate sleeping quarters for the owners' three children and guests. The biggest wow factor comes at the entry, from a plywood-latticework gazebo that arches over a lava plinth surrounded by water. Beyond is the main pavilion, which unfolds via a teak-wrapped breezeway running through the center of the complex and culminating in a reflecting pool.

Along this indoor-outdoor corridor, 9-foot-high windows offer views of the living area, capped in a domed cedar ceiling referencing Hawaiian grass skirts. The breezy decor—an off-white linen-covered Antonio Citterio sectional, a striped Andrée Putman rug—are the work of Meg Joannides, principal of MLK Studio and frequent Belzberg collaborator. Pragmatism guided the selection of materials, an array of sustainable and indigenous finishes that stand up well to humidity and moisture. Good thing: At the great room's far end, a glass wall opens up completely to access a teak lanai and an infinity-edge lap pool.

Clockwise from top left: *The powder room is dressed in an outsize orchid mosaic. In the kitchen, sustainably harvested walnut cabinetry is topped with counters of crystallized glass and stainless steel. A stepped frame of saw-cut basalt enfolds the teak-clad breezeway, which slopes into a reflecting pool.*

Clockwise from top left: *Cedar strips form the living room canopy's complex curves; a plasma-screen TV slides out of a stacked basalt wall. The structure of the plywood parabola*

was made from a kit of 600 parts manufactured in L.A., shipped across the Pacific, and assembled into an arch. The hallway leading to the master suite looks onto an outdoor shower. ➤

"The client wanted a series of pods and a strong visual element pointing to the sea on one side, the volcano on the other"

—HAGY BELZBERG

1 GAZEBO

2 SCREENING ROOM

3 KITCHEN

4 LIVING AREA

5 DINING AREA

6 MASTER SUITE

7 GUEST QUARTERS

8 CHILDREN'S QUARTERS

0   20   40   80

Clockwise from top left: *Behind the house is an infinity-edge lap pool. The master bedroom is topped by a cedar ceiling canopy and walled in glazed corner panels that slide open, providing direct access to the great outdoors. A guest room is furnished with a custom bed inside a teak frame. A teak vanity presides in the master bath.*

PROJECT TEAMS BARRY GARTIN; ANDREW ATWOOD; DAN RENTSCH; DAVID CHEUNG; BROCK DESMIT; CHRIS ARNTZEN; AARON LEPPANEN; PHIL LEE; CORY TAYLOR; LAUREN ZUZACK; JUSTIN BRECHTEL (BELZBERG ARCHITECTS); CHANTAL SPANICCIATI; SEYIE PUTSURE; REBECCA ROLLINS (MLK STUDIO)

PHOTOGRAPHY BENNY CHAN/FOTOWORKS

www.belzbergarchitects.com; www.mlkstudio.com

SURFSIDE RESIDENCE, MONTAUK, NEW YORK

Steven Harris Architects and Rees Roberts + Partners

HONOREE RESORT HOUSE

Steven Harris grew up at the beach in northeast Florida. So when a New York couple hired his firm to design a modern summer house atop tall ocean bluffs in Montauk, on New York's Long Island, Harris drew on cherished childhood memories of coastal life.

One such memory was of oceanfront houses in his hometown that each had a separate street-facing garage; the shady garden between the two structures was cooler and more sheltered than the lawn overlooking the water. Here, that recollection gave rise to a sheltered courtyard-entry garden for dining and lounging. There's no official front door; instead, oversize sliding-glass panels allow a clear sight line from the courtyard through the public rooms to the ocean beyond. Glide open the panels and the connection between courtyard and sea is even more immediate.

Materials were chosen to withstand the elements: ipe-frame windows and a durable dolomitic American limestone terrace that echoes the travertine floor inside. The spare decor by Rees Roberts + Partners combines built-ins and beach-friendly modernist furnishings like Ron Arad's Tom Vac plastic shell chairs.

The 5,000-square-foot house tucks four bedrooms and a convertible study into a pair of perpendicularly stacked volumes. Harris cantilevered the living room over a swimming pool to channel a Neutra-inspired Taylor Hardwick house next door to where his aunt lived in Florida. Lower-level underwater windows complete the cool maritime vibe.

Clockwise from top left: Gino Sarfatti's Triennale floor lamp stands in a glazed corner of the master bedroom. The study is one of two lower-level rooms with views into the swimming pool. Double-glazed ipe-frame sliding doors link the living and dining areas to the swimming pool. ➤

*Clockwise from far
left:* *The travertine-
floored living area
opens onto a garden
courtyard with the
pool and the sea
beyond. A skylight in
the master suite
creates the illusion
that the shower is
outdoors. The kitchen
and dining area
features Tom Vac*

PROJECT TEAMS ELIOT LEE; TOM ZOOK; BILL GREAVES (STEVEN HARRIS ARCHITECTS);
KATE RIZZO (REES ROBERTS + PARTNERS)
PHOTOGRAPHY SCOTT FRANCES

www.stevenharrisarchitects.com; www.reesroberts.com

*shell chairs and
a mid-century
chandelier. The
volume housing the
master suite shades
the ground-floor
living area.*

MAGNI DESIGN

PROJECT Residence, Jackson, Wyoming
STANDOUT The canopy's steel structure and tongue-
and-groove cedar slats repeat in the great room—
with the addition of bronze-framed pendant fixtures
PHOTOGRAPHY Matthew Millman

www.magnidesign.com

SPG ARCHITECTS

PROJECT Residence, Leicester, North Carolina
STANDOUT Stone and *cumaru* wood lend heft to an
exterior that's lightened by window walls facing
the Blue Ridge Mountains
PHOTOGRAPHY Daniel Levin

www.spgarchitects.com

emma gardner design

contemporary heirlooms • fine hand-made rugs

We are honored to be recognized by the design community.

Congratulations to the entire Best of the Year "Class" of 2011.

rebound - mixed grapes
© emma gardner design, llc

For more Information and our showrooms: www.emmagardnerdesign.com or toll free 1.877.377.3144

All rugs are produced with no child labor and certified by GOODWEAVE

D'Apostrophe Design

WINNER RURAL HOUSE

WEEKEND HOUSE, REMSENBURG, NEW YORK

Clockwise from left:
The living room's
existing beams
were enlarged by
recladding them in
oak salvaged from
a 300-year-old
Canadian barn. The
floorboards as well as
the staircase treads
and risers are wide-
plank Douglas fir. The
designer added new
aluminum-framed
windows and doors.
The staircase's angled
balustrades are
painted drywall. The
exterior was upgraded
with cedar planks
salvaged from a 200-
year-old barn.

D'Apostrophe Principal Francis D'Haene met Vincent Herbert, the Le Pain Quotidien bakery chain's CEO, when they were growing up in Belgium; both later moved to New York. Herbert's young family now spends weekends in a sleepy hamlet, in a faux barn built in the 1980's but clad in 300-year-old siding. D'Haene left most of the reclaimed planks intact but added hemlock and white pine around new doors and windows. The dialogue between old and new continues with the windows' plain glass and simple aluminum frames—replacing mullioned versions on all but the front facade—as well as a 5,500-square-foot interior that verges on monastic. He demolished walls to establish a loftlike sweep culminating in a 28-foot-high living area, where he bulked up the skimpy ceiling beams by applying antique barn siding of Douglas fir, spruce, and pine. From the living area, a staircase with balustrades folded origami-style ascends to three bedrooms, two bathrooms, and an open-plan master suite. The suite's bluestone flooring is the quietest of inside jokes: It's Belgian.

PROJECT TEAM KEVIN ESTRADA; OLGA BUKUR

PHOTOGRAPHY GREGORY HOLM

www.dapostrophe.com

RETREAT, ELAPHITE ISLANDS, CROATIA

Steven Harris Architects and Rees Roberts + Partners

WINNER RURAL HOUSE

For decades, architect Steven Harris and designer Lucien Rees Roberts—both *Interior Design* Hall of Fame members—have worked and lived together. Home is a New York loft; holidays and all of August take place northwest of Dubrovnik, on an island in the Elafiti Archipelago. The latter proved a liberating creative exercise for the designers, who had an opportunity to completely overhaul the property—a cluster of four 15th-century structures built from local stone.

Those original stone walls are just about all that remain of the time-ravaged original buildings, as the designers opened up the interiors to take advantage of water views and coax in sunlight and cool breezes. Newly installed finishes designed to blend with the historic envelope preserve the old-world charm: handmade Tuscan terra-cotta tiles, lime-washed ash floors, gray-stained wood ceiling beams, and antiqued cast-iron door handles. Other details are truly historic, such as a 15th-century stone gutter reborn as a bathroom sink.

Harris and Rees Roberts also brought in more up-to-date elements, such as the living room's mammoth steel fireplace hood and cast-concrete window seat. Like the homeowners, the furnishings are modern, international sophisticates: Eero Saarinen Executive chairs in the dining room, a Pierre Paulin Ribbon lounge in the master bedroom, and Jorge Zalszupin rosewood armchairs in the living room.

Clockwise from top left: Jorge Zalszupin's rosewood Dinamarquesa armchairs have pride of place in the living room, which has a view of the water from a concrete window seat. The main structure—a 1,500-square-foot former merchant's home—is one of four on the property. A 1966 Pierre Paulin Ribbon chair perches in the master bedroom. ➤

The sculptural steel fireplace hood above the open hearth was handmade in Croatia. The designers exposed and restored the home's original stone walls, which date to the 15th century. ➣

Clockwise from far left: A view into the living room reveals a linen-covered sofa and vintage driftwood table. The guest room's vintage Paul McCobb ottoman was reupholstered in curly lamb. An old barn was converted into a painting studio with sliding glass panels. Dorothy Thorpe Lucite lamps flank the bed in the

master suite. The house is sited on a hill overlooking a harbor. ➤

PROJECT TEAMS ANTONIO ZANINOVIC (STEVEN HARRIS ARCHITECTS);
DAVID KELLY (REES ROBERTS + PARTNERS)

PHOTOGRAPHY SCOTT FRANCES

www.stevenharrisarchitects.com; www.reesroberts.com

"Sophisticated furnishings hold their place as modern sculptures"
—STEVEN HARRIS

Clockwise from far left: Eero Saarinen Executive chairs pull up to a cerused-oak dining table supported by bronze bases; the Lucite candlesticks were designed by Dorothy Thorpe in the 1970's. A bathroom sink was made from a 15th-century stone gutter. Ancient beams recycled from a house in the village form the pergola.

WEEKEND RETREAT, STRATTON, VERMONT

The design-review committee for tiny Stratton, Vermont, demands what some call "contextual" residential architecture. Commissioned to dream up a client's weekend getaway, Shamir Shah—whose style is decidedly au courant—had no desire to supply a boilerplate log-cabin fantasy. But chances were nonexistent that the town would approve a modernist house on a steep ½-acre mountainside site.

So the New York–based Shah set out on a back-road bicycle tour armed with his camera to explore the state's architectural vernacular. He went to the drawing board thoroughly inspired by the magnificent historic barns he'd photographed on the trip. The result: a 6,000-square-foot, six-bedroom house with simple massing capped by a standing-seam roof of powder-coated galvanized steel. Thanks to black-stained cedar siding and an ambitious landscape restoration using native plants, the resulting house meshes with the Vermont mountainside like the cherished old barns it evokes.

Clean contemporary interiors frame views of the woodland. The main floor serves as a loftlike entertainment space, with an open kitchen that flows into a great room. Two suites—a master plus one for guests—occupy the upper floor. The lower level has eight bunks, an enormous playroom, and storage for ski equipment—which comes in rather handy, since slopes traverse the woods on both sides of the house.

PROJECT TEAM ROBERT BLUE; ORN RAJSIRISONGSRI; ARKAIDIY EBER
PHOTOGRAPHY ANTOINE BOOTZ
www.shamirshahdesign.com

Shamir Shah Design

HONOREE **RURAL HOUSE**

THE MODERN FARMHOUSE, EAST HAMPTON, NEW YORK

Elke Griffith spearheads a line of women's sportswear and her husband, Jerome, is CEO of American luggage manufacturer Tumi. Perhaps it's no surprise that these branding pros dreamed up a nickname for their vacation home: TMF, short for the Modern Farmhouse.

The contemporary take on country life was the duo's fifth collaboration with principal Betty Wasserman. The interior design draws from the 6,500-square-foot house's close-to-the-ocean setting and silvery architectural stonework. Outside, what appears to be weathered-wood paneling is newly installed to evoke both beaches and barns. Inside, Wasserman dressed everything from windows to seating in layers of restful neutrals—from putty to ecru to greige.

The house offers three living rooms, including a sitting area warmed by a fireplace. Furnishings include a Chris Lehreke floor lamp, Vladimir Kagan sofas, and John Wigmore's conical pendants made from Japanese paper. Since many floors are exquisite stone or wood, Wasserman strictly limited rugs underfoot; the few she used anchor vignettes in living areas or give occupants soft landings in the five bedrooms.

Wasserman, who started her career as an art dealer, took her clients on studio visits to expand their collections. Among the 30 new works are several by local artists: Soraida Bedoya contributed a porcelain wall installation. Gary Gissler was commissioned to interview the couple, then add words from those conversations onto his canvas portrait of them. And Joel Perlman erected a monumental steel sculpture that sits poolside. Contemplating contemporary art while swimming laps? How very modern.

Betty Wasserman Art & Interiors

HONOREE RURAL HOUSE

Clockwise from top left: A cluster of Japanese rice paper pendants by John Wigmore illuminates the living room. Reflecting pools flank the walkway to the entry. A Helenbilt Silver Lining Upstream pendant hangs over the custom walnut-slab dining table; the oil on canvas was painted by the owners' neighbor. ➣

Clockwise from top left: *The exterior of the house, by architect Bruce D. Nagel, is clad in gray-stained wood siding. The den's existing chimney was painted white. A glass-*

walled staircase leads to a loft. The loft overlooks the den, furnished with a large-loop rug and walnut coffee table. A seating area off the kitchen features a Minotti sectional and Warren Platner cocktail table. Sculptor Joel Perlman's Seven Ponds II, *in oxidized bronze, sits beside the pool.*

"Since the house is near the beach, we wanted the palette to be light and white and creamy"

Wasserman added a bluestone surround to the living room's existing fireplace and reclad the hearth in recycled wood planks. A Soraida Bedoya porcelain piece hangs behind one of two Vladimir Kagan sofas.

Clockwise from top left: In the master bedroom, calfskin table lamps perch on Christian Liaigre nightstands built from sycamore and ebonized cherry; the walnut bench is by Jens Risom. An L-shape lap pool wraps the rear of the house. Limestone floor tiles run below a free-standing fiberglass tub in the master bathroom, furnished with a faux-leather armchair. In a garret guest bedroom, a skylight is fitted with

PHOTOGRAPHY ERIC STRIFLER

www.bettywasserman.com

a plantation shutter stained gray to match the painted-wood ceiling.

Ghislaine Viñas
Interior Design

WINNER URBAN HOUSE

Clockwise from left: The design includes kid-friendly elements such as vinyl-upholstered dining chairs and primary colors. An oil on canvas by Lisa Ruyter brightens the kitchen. A blown-glass chandelier by Suzan Etkin hangs over a pair of wool-covered sofas in the living area; the foam sculpture in the stairwell is by Jason Rogenes. ➤

TRIBECA RESIDENCE, NEW YORK

A perfect meeting of minds between designer and client resulted in this home for a family of five. No wonder the two are so simpatico: This is the *sixth* project Ghislaine Viñas has completed for Paige West, who owns the Chelsea gallery Mixed Greens. In addition to colorful personalities and a love of contemporary art, the two also share a passion for high-wattage hues and no-holds-barred furnishings.

The 8,000-square-foot home is spread over the top four floors of a six-story TriBeCa building, a former warehouse built in 1915. The structure was overhauled by architect Peter Guthrie of DDG Partners, a real-estate development firm whose management team includes West's husband. Guthrie's gut renovation left only the original joists untouched, giving Viñas carte blanche on the interiors—which meant supersaturated finishes and furnishings plus brazen artwork to match. In the kitchen, Lisa Ruyter's primary-hued oil on canvas inspired accents such as the painted island cabinetry and custom-tinted solid-surfacing counter in yolk yellow. A guest bedroom outfitted in zingy gray-and-white stripes gets electric-green accents. A photograph of a parakeet sparked the palette for the study, lit by a massive pendant dome sprouting electric-blue feathers and featuring white shelves backed in turquoise and sulfur-yellow wallpaper. Even the books are organized by color—well-read meets, well, *red.*

PROJECT TEAMS VANÉ BROUSSARD; GIOVANNA SGUERA; KARINA DHARMAZI; MANDI MARSH; ANDREA DOVALLE; STEPHANIE SHEPHERD; SOPHIE BERNHARDT; ABBY SAVAGE (GHISLAINE VIÑAS INTERIOR DESIGN); JES PAONE; CHRIS NOGOY; STEPHANIE KIM; KATHERYN SALAZAR (DDG PARTNERS)

PHOTOGRAPHY ERIC LAIGNEL

www.gvinteriors.com; www.ddgpartners.com

Clockwise from top left: The study features cotton-covered armchairs and a feathered pendant dome by Benjamin Noriega-Ortiz and Steven Wine. A Vik Muniz photograph adds an arty touch to the boys' library. Custom neon clouds brighten their bathroom.

The Mark Mulroney mural in the boys' bedroom was inspired by The Adventures of Tom Sawyer. *Piero Lissoni and Carlo Tamborini designed the guest room chair.*

STUDIO MK27

PROJECT São Paulo, Brazil
STANDOUT Folding teak screens open up both ends of a volume predominantly built with textured raw concrete
PHOTOGRAPHY Nelson Kon
www.marciokogan.com.br

ISAY WEINFELD

PROJECT São Paulo, Brazil
STANDOUT Adjoining concrete structures were sited to embrace new patios while respecting old-growth trees
PHOTOGRAPHY Leonardo Finotti
www.isayweinfeld.com

XTEN ARCHITECTURE

PROJECT Encino, California
STANDOUT A trapezoid that juts out from a 1960's ranch house, this addition combines steel and concrete with glass coated in a nano-ceramic film to protect artwork inside
PHOTOGRAPHY Art Gray
www.xtenarchitecture.com

SPACE.
REINVENTED.

SWING CHAISE SOFA/QUEEN WALL BED

New York

Toronto

Vancouver

Victoria

SEE OUR WEBSITE FOR 40 MORE
TRANSFORMING SYSTEMS
MADE IN ITALY BY CLEI

RESOURCE FURNITURE

SPACE. REINVENTED.

969 Third Avenue @ 58th Street
New York, NY 10022
212 753 2039
www.resourcefurniture.com

DAVID YURMAN, NEW YORK

Turning an Italianate town house into a flagship for David Yurman jewelry, *Interior Design* Hall of Fame member Michael Gabellini and partner Kimberly Sheppard discovered that the scope of the project included not just a 6,000-square-foot location but also a brand reinvention. The top two levels were relegated to offices, while the lower three are dedicated to a boutique that encompasses women's, men's, bridal, and couture collections. Staggered voids create vertical flow and what Gabellini describes as a "Rubik's Cube of complexity and delight." Materials such as cast bronze, walnut, striated gray marble, hand-troweled plaster, and gray-painted canvas establish a muted luxury. And the pièce de résistance is the skylit staircase. Cantilevered walnut treads and stainless-steel risers spiral around a cascade of stainless-steel rods, a reference to both Yurman's cable bracelets and Harry Bertoia's sound sculptures. As for the glass balustrade, its hexagonal shape was inspired by the cut of gems.

Gabellini Sheppard Associates

WINNER RETAIL / FASHION

PROJECT TEAM DANIEL GARBOWIT; ELINA CARDET; OZLEM ACKAY; STACEY BERTIN; TOMOKO HIROSE; KENTARO ISHIHARA; TOMOMI NARITA; JONGKU YEE

PHOTOGRAPHY PAUL WARCHOL

www.gabellinisheppard.com

Clockwise from far left: Slatted ceilings of American walnut distinguish the ground level and the men's salon one flight up. A proscenium of limestone and Cor-Ten steel frames the lower two levels of the 19th-century town house. The men's salon features aubergine silk carpets and bronze-silk mirror wainscoting. A glass-enclosed staircase alternating slabs of walnut and stainless steel rises through the rear atrium, spiraling around ceiling-hung stainless-steel rods.

CHRISTIAN LOUBOUTIN, MIAMI

212box

HONOREE RETAIL / FASHION

Over the years, shoe guru Christian Louboutin has entrusted the design of 36 boutiques to 212box principal Eric Clough. At the recently opened Miami Design District location, the architect managed to tuck 2,400 square feet behind a coral-stone facade draped with orchids, giving those who enter a teaser of the hothouse vibe within.

Visitors step into a concrete-floored foyer that doubles as an art gallery. A wall to the left incorporates a wood-tile mosaic that spells out in Braille-derivative symbols a Lyn Hejinian poem. For the shop's grand opening, artist Madeleine Berkhemer created a site-specific installation: A red spiderweb of ripped stockings spiked with Louboutin heels beckons provocatively from the ceiling. And with one-way-mirror walls, Clough transforms the very act of shopping into performance art, allowing viewers to peep voyeuristically onto the sales floor via display niches showcasing the brand's signature crimson-sole stilettos.

Clockwise from top left: An art installation by sculptor Madeleine Berkhemer features a Christian Louboutin stiletto ensnared in a web of stockings. The sales floor is lit by a glass chandelier from the shoe designer's personal collection; Eva Ionesco shot the photo of Louboutin. Arched display niches were designed to mimic dovecotes. ➤

Inside, flooring segues to broadloom in the same brazen red while the ceiling and cash-wrap are collages of salvaged tin. Mosaic tiles are used here, too, displaying a mix of 32 world languages and symbols drawn by Clough's 12-year-old nephew. Somewhere within the shop, the designer also concealed an installation by Taylor Moore, a 19-year-old Brooklyn artist. Though Clough hesitates to discuss it (the better to preserve the mystery), clues to its location can be found in the tiles.

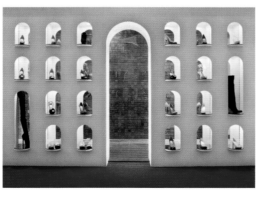

Clockwise from far left: *Shoppers try on shoes in the comfort of a Bokja Couture chair clad in a patchwork of recycled Lebanese textiles. A swath of ceramic hieroglyphic tiles was hand-set into a display wall. A strategically placed mirror fosters the illusion that the*

banquette is twice as long. The sales floor's reclaimed-tin ceiling tiles were sourced throughout New England. ➤

"Could we capture the moment of a woman shopping for shoes, then hang that on a hook as art?"

Shoppers enter an L-shape foyer turned gallery animated by Berkhemer's installation and floored with polished concrete. One-way mirrors wall off the sales floor and offer a peek inside. ⬎

1 ENTRY
2 GALLERY
3 SALES AREAS
4 BACK OF HOUSE

0 5 10 20

PROJECT TEAM DAVID MAGID; MORI BUSTER
PHOTOGRAPHY ERIC LAIGNEL
www.212box.com

Clockwise from left:
Broadloom carpet in Louboutin red anchors a Bokja Bean sofa upholstered in recycled textiles. The orchids on the oolite facade are wired in place so their roots will take hold in the stone's pores. Reclaimed tin tiles also face the cash-wrap counter.

YABU PUSHELBERG

PROJECT Bay, Toronto
STANDOUT This department store's luxury St. Regis Room is now simply the Room, defined by screens built from stainless steel, lacquered plywood, and acrylic
PHOTOGRAPHY Evan Dion
www.yabupushelberg.com

ISAY WEINFELD

PROJECT Carina Duek, São Paulo, Brazil
STANDOUT Vintage wooden wardrobes line the two-level boutique as well as the showroom on the top story
PHOTOGRAPHY Leonardo Finotti
www.isayweinfeld.com

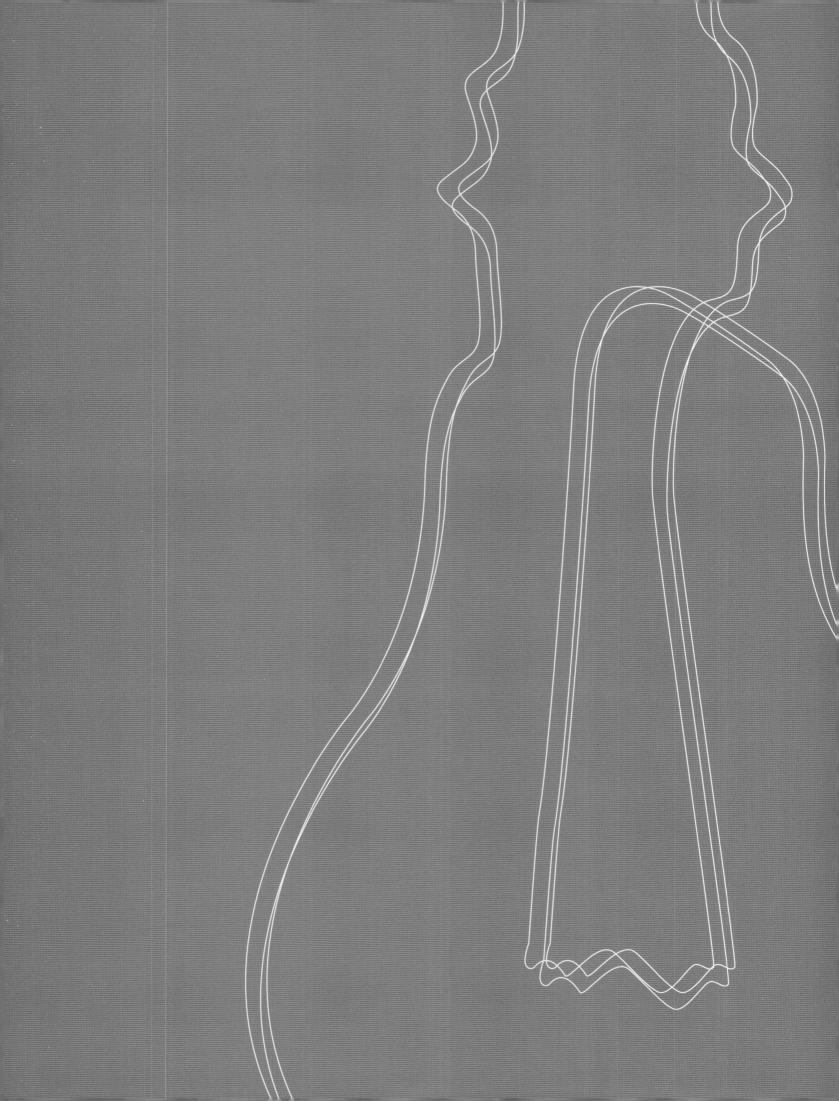

VICTOR CHURCHILL, WOOLLAHRA, AUSTRALIA

Dreamtime Australia Design

WINNER RETAIL

The exquisitely marbled lamb chop displayed in a bell jar—with 18 surveillance cameras trained on it—says everything you need to know about Victor Churchill: The butchery's meats are as coveted as fine jewelry, and its aesthetic is delectably tongue in cheek.

The decor, by Dreamtime principal Michael McCann, is at once high-class and high-concept. Materials like book-matched Calacatta marble, copper, and pecan-wood veneer confer old-world grace while an irreverent aesthetic keeps the tone unfussily fresh. Most notably, the firm forsook the customary division between front and back of house, opting to showcase the fine art of butchering. A full-height glass wall is all that separates the sales floor from a refrigerated room where pristine cuts of meat and poultry are carved on a trio of barrel-size oak cylinders. A sandstone wall, unearthed during renovation, serves as a backdrop to the action. Backlit Himalayan salt bricks play a similar role in the adjacent cool room where meats age on a revolving rack. Opposite, custom copper-front refrigerators hold steaks and chops as well as pâtés and terrines prepared on-site. And the designers didn't shy from getting saucy with the details: The drawer pulls and door handles, cast in bronze, resemble sausages.

Clockwise from left: The painted-timber facade offers a view inside via a glass-enclosed meats refrigerator. The drawer pulls are copper-finished cast-bronze. The special of the day is showcased in a bell-jar vitrine supported by a Calacatta marble base affixed to a pecano-veneered wall. ➤

Clockwise from above: *The mosaic floor was cut from book-matched slabs of Calacatta marble; refrigerated copper cabinets house raw meats alongside prepared foods. Cured meats hang in a nook clad in pecano veneer—the same wood treatment used throughout. Butchers prepare meat and poultry on French oak cutting blocks illuminated by fiber-optic spotlights. All handles and pulls mimic sausage links.* ➤

"The client suggested breaking all the rules— yet respecting them at the same time"

Clockwise from top left: *In the cool room, an onyxlike wall of Himalayan salt bricks is illuminated from behind. For hygiene and health-code purposes, the sandstone rubble wall discovered during renovation is covered in glass; a museum-quality antique Berkel meat slicer has pride of place on the retail floor. Hand-carved copper fretwork fronts the charcuterie counter.* ➤

PROJECT TEAM MICHAEL McCANN;
SALLY GORDON; TIM BARRY
PHOTOGRAPHY PAUL GOSNEY
www.dreamtimeaustraliadesign.com

***Clockwise from top
left:*** *A grouping of
18 copper-sheathed
surveillance cameras
(only four of which are
operable) keep vigil at
the glass vitrine. The
restroom wallpaper
features a raw-meat
print. A photomural
of the company
founders marks the
entry to the private
dining room. There,
patrons sit on
benches crafted
from European beech
butcher block that
surround a communal
table.*

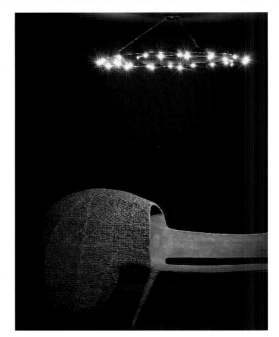

Agence Néonata

HONOREE RETAIL

GALERIE BSL, PARIS, FRANCE

Béatrice Saint-Laurent considers the northern Marais a mecca for cutting-edge art and design. Hence, the former publicist chose that neighborhood to launch her Galerie BSL, which commissions and showcases contemporary design objects alongside rare vintage jewelry and lighting. To complement avant-garde work by the likes of Ettore Sottsass, Gae Aulenti, and *Interior Design* Hall of Famers Ingo Maurer and Matteo Thun, Saint-Laurent chose to radically rethink the archetypal boutique. No podiums or spinning racks here—she imagined something closer to *2001: A Space Odyssey.*

Enter principal Noé Duchaufour-Lawrance, of Agence Néonata, who set about redefining the ground floor of a modest 18th-century building that once housed workshops. The floor plan funnels from 17 feet in front to 12 feet at the rear, where a skylight caps an enclosed former courtyard to create an illuminated sweep of space. Duchaufour-Lawrance darkened everything else, ebonizing the oak floor and painting walls and exposed pipes anthracite gray. A seamless swath of white solid-surfacing now unfurls from the entry. Beginning as a low display platform, the ribbon dips along the floor then climbs a sidewall, folding at the ceiling to form a canopy. This element, reminiscent of a crashing wave, provides a striking backdrop for rotating solo shows. Other collectibles—such as mid-century Japanese lamps and a jumble of Nacho Carbonell foam giraffes—are displayed on lacquered shelves and in a constellation of petite wall-mounted vitrines.

Clockwise from left: *On a sidewall, jewelry and small design objects are showcased in vitrines lit by LEDs. Spanish designer Nacho Carbonell's seating rests at the rear of the gallery. Also at the rear, a skylight protects the former courtyard, now treated to a swoop of Corian.* ➤

From left: *The solid-surfacing element starts as a display platform before curling down along the floor and taking a turn up to form a wall and ceiling canopy. Walls, floor, exposed pipes, and other obtrusive structural details got coated in gray to make them recede.*

PROJECT TEAM LLUC GIROS
PHOTOGRAPHY ERIC LAIGNEL
www.noeduchaufourlawrance.com

ONE PLUS PARTNERSHIP

PROJECT Kubrick Bookshop, Beijing, China

STANDOUT Powder-coated steel appears everywhere from the display modules to the pivoting panels that close off the cash register and membership counter

PHOTOGRAPHY Ajax Law Ling Kit and Virginia Lung/One Plus Partnership

www.onepluspartnership.com

MINISTRY OF DESIGN

PROJECT Prologue, Singapore

STANDOUT Customers encounter bookcases clad in plastic laminate before taking the epoxy-finished steel stairs up to the stationery department

PHOTOGRAPHY Edward Hendricks/CI&A Photography

www.modonline.com

MARKZEFF

PROJECT Brother & Sister, Hong Kong

STANDOUT Peruse the decorative objects, jewelry, and limited-edition sneakers, all showcased in vitrines with burnished-bronze frames, or digest it all in the café

PHOTOGRAPHY Olaf Mueller

www.markzeff.com

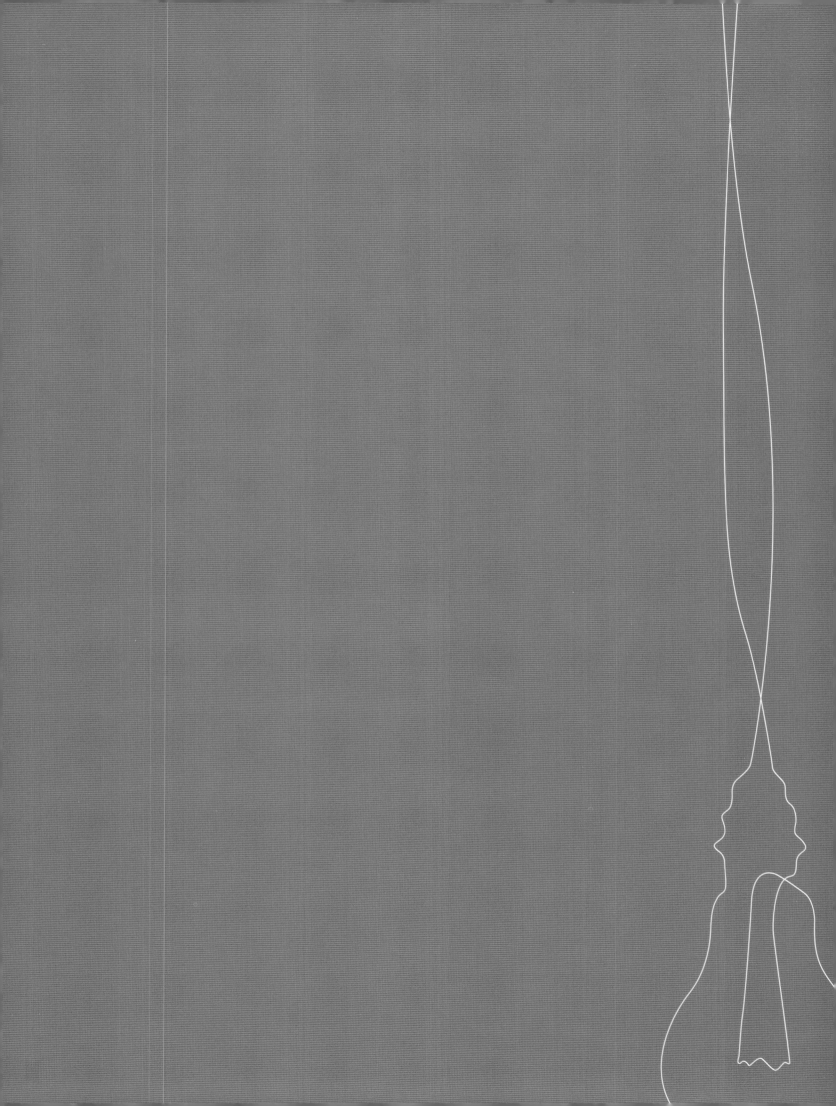

AVENUE ROAD, TORONTO

Yabu Pushelberg

WINNER SHOWROOM

How do you showcase a range of furniture, lighting, and textiles by global luminaries from Eileen Gray to Konstantin Grcic—being all things to all potential customers while still reflecting a unique retail program? George Yabu and Glenn Pushelberg's solution is a gallerylike setting with simple symmetry. They inserted a long skylight right down the middle of the three-story redbrick structure, the former Consumers' Gas Company, built in 1852. Vignettes hug the perimeter while blackened-steel frames accessory-display cases that appear to float along the sides of the central atrium. On the lower level, a glass-fronted conference room is furnished with Jorge Zalszupin's chairs and a table by Helmut Jahn and Yorgo Lykouria. Staff members spend most of the time, however, in the serene open office found at the back of the top level, tucked beneath the original ceiling trusses.

Clockwise from top left: The lower level's conference room is fronted in glass. Crafted from blackened steel and glass, vitrines housing small objets line the atrium. The historic gas company building dates to the 19th century. The main showroom is floored in polished concrete.

PROJECT TEAM ALEX EDWARD; ALIENOR GUILHEM; AMY LAW;
ASHLEY RUMSEY; CALLAND LEE; SHANE PARK; STEFANIE FOISSEY; TAMMY TAI;
TATIANA CHEVELEVA; VERONICA SMITH

PHOTOGRAPHY EVAN DION

www.yabupushelberg.com

Clockwise from top left: An adhesive vinyl image of the founder of the company that became Flavor Paper dominates the printing studio. A canopy of polished stainless steel cantilevers 8 feet beyond the entrance. Hand-screening takes place in the studio, at vacuum tables 52 feet long; the mirror above hides the HVAC systems. Neon flowers in the light well, enclosed in tempered glass, are based on the Sakura pattern papering the adjacent stairwell. Custom spinning racks in the showroom are polished aluminum.

FLAVOR PAPER, BROOKLYN, NEW YORK

When Jon Sherman decided to move Flavor Paper from New Orleans to Brooklyn, New York, he called Skylab principal Jeff Kovel. The chosen site was a 1931 brick garage encompassing 19,000 square feet. In addition to improving the manufacturing conditions, the new headquarters was to act as the supreme marketing vehicle. "Everywhere we could, we three-dimensionalized Flavor Paper and pattern in general," Kovel says. A ground-level studio allows passersby to view the manufacturing process. Level two is the lounge-y showroom, where wallpaper is displayed like artwork in huge polished-aluminum spinning racks. Kovel abstracted one particular pattern for the inlays in the terrazzo, and another pattern inspired the round ceiling coves and the serpentine banquette. The building-as-marketing-tool strategy is perhaps best executed by the former car lift. Its three windows frame highly visible pink and purple neon blow-up versions of a Flavor Paper floral, which seems to ascend the 58-foot-high shaft like an electric vine.

Skylab Architecture

WINNER SHOWROOM

PROJECT TEAM KENT HELI; KIM KOVEL; CECILY RYAN; MATT GEIGER; DANIEL MEYERS; CHRISTOPHER BROWN; DANNON CANTERBURY; BRENT GRUBB; DRU UELTSCHI

PHOTOGRAPHY ERIC LAIGNEL (1-3, 5); BOONE SPEED (4)

www.skylabdesign.com

KRIS LIN INTERIOR DESIGN

PROJECT Yong Nian, Xiamen, China
STANDOUT Origami inspired this real-estate developer's showroom for a residential complex
PHOTOGRAPHY Zhao Yaodong

CLIVE WILKINSON ARCHITECTS

PROJECT Haworth, Chicago
STANDOUT Ronan & Erwan Bouroullec's Clouds are cool blue, while panel systems, columns, and ottomans flaunt red, pink, and orange
PHOTOGRAPHY Elizabeth Fraiberg/E3 Photography
www.clivewilkinson.com

best of year snaps

Interior Design magazine's Best of Year Awards, familiarly known as the BoYs, brought 800 attendees to the lobby of New York's IAC Building by Gehry Partners.

1. Interior Design president **Mark Strauss** and editor in chief **Cindy Allen** kicking off the ceremony.

2. Esti Barnes, design director of Rug winner Top Floor, and Budget winner **Johnson Chou.**

3. **Lee Mindel** of Shelton, Mindel & Associates, winner for the Apartment category.

4. **Richard Shemtov,** whose company, Dune, won Seating/ Contract Guest for Pipeline, with its designer, **Harry Allen.**

5. **Francis D'Haene,** principal of Rural House winner D'Apostrophe Design, and his wife, Anaïs & I owner **Jane Yang.**

6. Interior Design associate publisher **Carol Cisco,** Hansgrohe president **Russ Wheeler,** and **Todd DeGarmo,** CEO of the Office Renovation winner, Studios Architecture.

7. Architectural designer **Andres Cova** and principal **Eric Gartner** of SPG Architects, which was honored in the Resort House category.

8. Interior Design Hall of Fame member **Karim Rashid,** whose firm tied for first in Health Care and designed two winning products, for Alloy and Vondom.

9. **Sina Pearson** of Sina Pearson Textiles, winner for Textiles/ Outdoor, getting a congratulatory hug from **Allen.**

10. **Dean Goodman** of Levitt Goodman Architects, winner for Institutional.

11. Victory for **Ghislaine Viñas,** the Urban House winner.

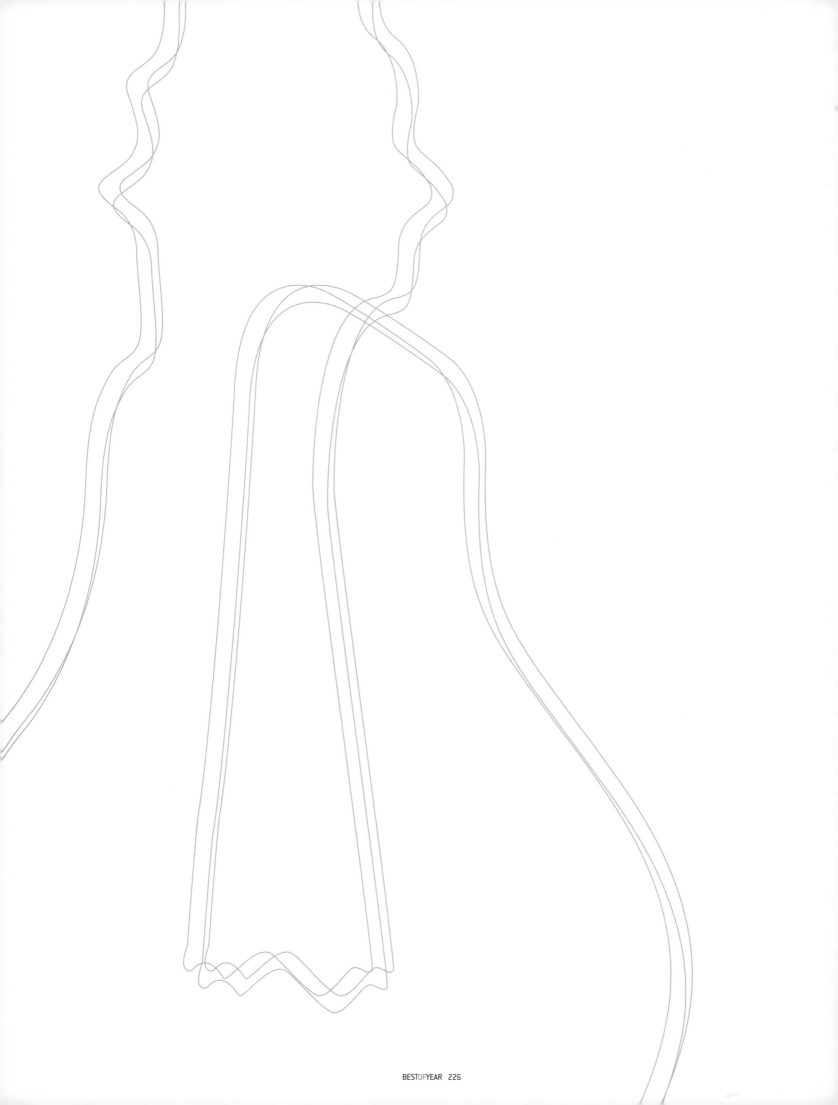

best of year

products

Ezequiel Farca

HONOREE ACCESSORIES

Mexico City–based firm Ezequiel Farca explains that it taps into a "profound understanding of personal needs and behaviors" to create its highly integrated, experiential designs for hospitality and residential projects. But there's one gem the company kept all to itself: a set of crockery originally designed for the showroom and now available to the public. Plates, soup bowls, plus coffee and espresso cups in high-fire, matte earthenware look entirely contemporary but have a primitive, sensual edge. We can't wait to get our hands on them.

PRODUCT EF crockery
DESIGNER Ezequiel Farca
www.ezequielfarca.com

Nana Wall Systems

By definition, a wall equals permanence. Unless, of course, it's the SL82 structurally glazed folding-glass system. When closed, it mimics the expansiveness of an all-glass facade—a particularly palatable accompaniment for structurally glazed buildings. But a sprawling exterior opening emerges as the thermally insulated panels fold together, sliding on bottom-supported rollers across an optional single track. Suitable for commercial or residential applications up to 39 feet wide and incorporating a maximum of 12 panels, the assembly boasts a multipoint locking system to ensure optimum security.

PRODUCT SL82 structurally glazed folding-glass system
DESIGN Werner Helmich
www.nanawall.com

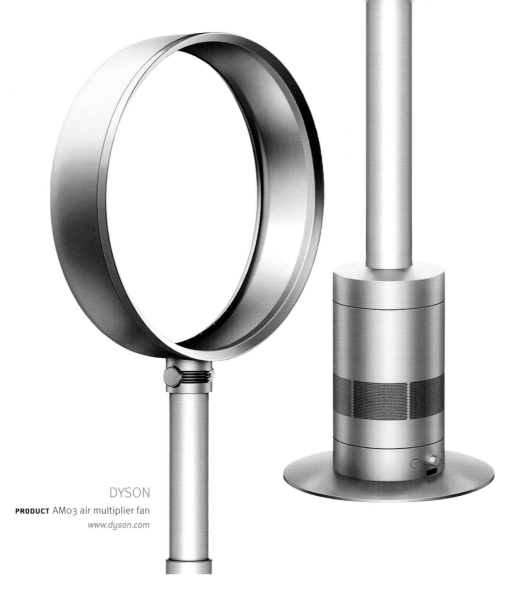

DYSON

PRODUCT AM03 air multiplier fan
www.dyson.com

HONOREES **ACCESSORIES**

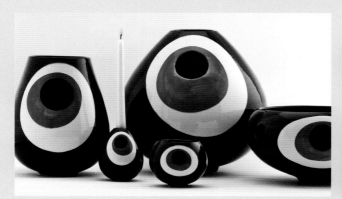

GAIA & GINO

PRODUCT Vases, bowls, and candleholder
COLLECTION Eye
DESIGN Sebastian Bergne
www.gaiagino.com

BONALDO

PRODUCT Pebble occasional table
DESIGN Matthias Demacker
www.bonaldo.it

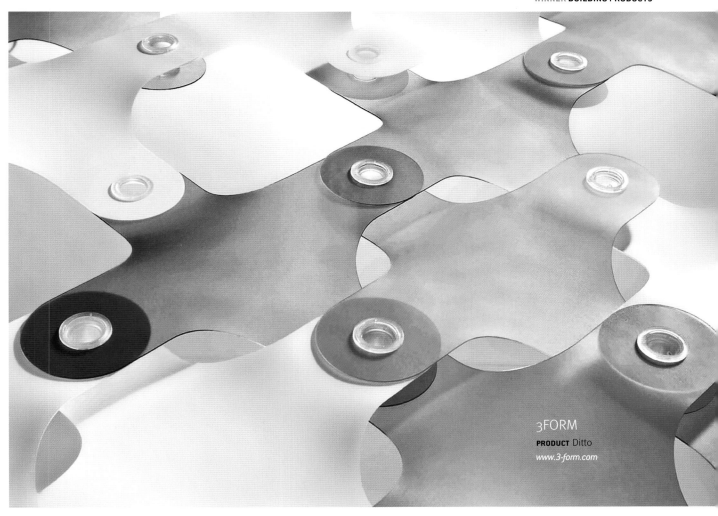

3FORM
PRODUCT Ditto
www.3-form.com

SPARK MODERN FIRES

PRODUCT Fire Ribbon Vent-Free Vu-Thru fireplace
www.sparkfires.com

SKYLINE DESIGN

PRODUCT Animals eco-friendly glass
COLLECTION Kids Glass
www.skydesign.com

SKYLINE DESIGN

PRODUCT Add On
COLLECTION Markerglass
DESIGN Suzanne Tick
www.skydesign.com

HONOREES ACCESSORIES / **OFFICE**

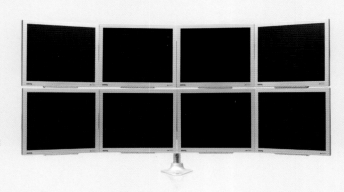

HUMANSCALE

PRODUCT Paramount monitor display
www.humanscale.com

COALESSE

PRODUCT Power Pod
COLLECTION SW-1
www.coalesse.com

HERMAN MILLER

PRODUCT Flo monitor arm
COLLECTION Thrive Portfolio
www.hermanmiller.com

CALIFORNIA FAUCETS

PRODUCT CeraLine linear shower drain with stainless-steel veneer

www.calfaucets.com

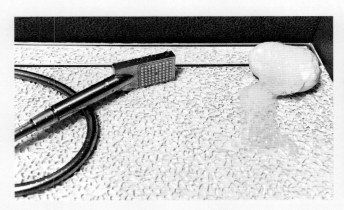

INFINITY DRAIN

PRODUCT TIF AS linear drain

www.infinitydrain.com

ALCHEMY GLASS & LIGHT

PRODUCT Alchemy Glow LED for undermount sinks

www.alchemyglass.com

WETSTYLE

PRODUCT Low-threshold shower receptor and shampoo niches
COLLECTION DC

www.wetstyle.ca

DORNBRACHT

PRODUCT Performing Shower
DESIGN Sieger Design
www.dornbracht.com

HONOREES **BATH FITTINGS**

WATERMARK DESIGNS

PRODUCT Brooklyn faucet
DESIGN Incorporated
www.watermark-designs.com

WEBERT ITALIAN DESIGN

PRODUCT Single-lever lavatory
COLLECTION Wolo
DESIGN Massimiliano Settimelli
www.webertusa.com

KOHLER CO.

PRODUCT Lavatory faucet
COLLECTION Karbon
www.kohler.com

RAPSEL

PRODUCT Larch soaking tub
COLLECTION Ofuro
DESIGN Matteo Thun and
Antonio Rodriguez
www.rapsel.it

HONOREES **BATH FIXTURES**

STONE FOREST

PRODUCT Adagio chaise lounge
COLLECTION Siena
www.stoneforest.com

AMERICAN STANDARD

PRODUCT EcoSilent whirlpool system
www.americanstandard-us.com

AXOR

PRODUCT Shower column
COLLECTION Axor Urquiola
DESIGN Patricia Urquiola
www.hansgrohe-usa.com

Carpet in high-traffic convention centers and office
towers rarely gets much notice; people are often in
too big a hurry. Domestic Alchemy should stop them
in their tracks. Edgy and enchanting, the collection was
inspired by stones, metals, and gems of different regions
of the U.S. Its flat-weave construction has a rich depth
of both texture and color—high-tech meets homespun.
Made of piece-dyed yarn, it's also designed to outperform
any competitor. And if it encourages people to slow
down, all the better.

Bentley Prince Street

WINNER CARPET / BROADLOOM

PRODUCT Domestic Alchemy broadloom
www.bentleyprincestreet.com

Top Floor Rugs

WINNER CARPET / RUGS

Esti Barnes, the founder and design director of London's Top Floor Rugs, is known for her bespoke creations that reveal a fascination with patterns found in nature. She brings together rich texture and ombré tones in Emmenthal, a hand-tufted, 100-percent-wool rug based on themes of decoupage. The flat surface of graduated browns is randomly perforated, terminating in edges that bring to mind a carpet (pun intended) of overlapping leaves. Each is made to order, so you may color—and shape—your world differently, should you so desire.

PRODUCT Emmenthal rug
DESIGN Esti Barnes
www.topfloorrugs.com

DURKAN

PRODUCT Work It Baby, Glam It Up, and Strike a Pose
COLLECTION On the Runway
www.durkan.com

SHAW CONTRACT GROUP

COLLECTION Social
www.shawcontractgroup.com

MANNINGTON COMMERCIAL

COLLECTION Undercurrent
www.mannington.com

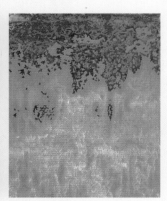

INDI-B

PRODUCT Ginko Wild
COLLECTION IndiB Home
www.indib.com

EMMA GARDNER DESIGN

PRODUCT Cream Rabbit
COLLECTION Rebound
DESIGN Emma Gardner
www.emmagardnerdesign.com

TAI PING CARPETS

PRODUCT Ephemera
COLLECTION Vestige
www.taipingcarpets.com

SHAW
CONTRACT GROUP

PRODUCT Overlay and Scale
COLLECTION 18X36
www.shawcontractgroup.com

LEES CARPETS

COLLECTION Digital Infusion
www.leescarpets.com

INTERFACEFLOR

PRODUCT Beale Street
and Union Avenue
DESIGN David Oakey
www.interfaceflor.com

VORWERK

COLLECTION Freescale
www.relative-space.com

BLANCO

PRODUCT Solon drop-in
compost management system

www.blancoamerica.com

LUTRON ELECTRONICS CO.

PRODUCT Dimmable CFL/LED dimmer

www.lutron.com

BUZZISPACE

PRODUCT Buzziskin
biodegradable 3-D wall tile

www.dapostrophe.net

SPINNEYBECK

PRODUCT Novus recycled leather

www.spinneybeck.com

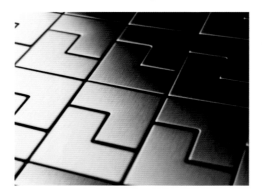

ALLOY

PRODUCT Metal tiles
COLLECTION Karim for Alloy
DESIGN Karim Rashid

www.alloydesign.com.au

HONOREES **FLOOR COVERING** / **HARD**

SA BAXTER

PRODUCT Bronze plank flooring

www.sabaxter.com

MANNINGTON
COMMERICIAL

PRODUCT Handcrafted
hardwood planks
COLLECTION Earthly Elements

www.mannington.com

USF CONTRACT

PRODUCT Bamboo Hues
strand-woven bamboo planks

www.usfcontract.com

ARTISTIC TILE

PRODUCT Ziva 3-D stone tile

www.artistictile.com

NEW RAVENNA MOSAICS

PRODUCT Ganesha stone mosaic

www.newravenna.com

NEMO TILE COMPANY

PRODUCT Viscaya Platino
electroplated-glass tile

www.nemotile.com

WALKER ZANGER

PRODUCT Mosaic in honed slate
and iridescent marbleized glass

COLLECTION Waterfall

www.walkerzanger.com

VITRA

COLLECTION ACSU storage units
DESIGN Antonio Citterio
www.vitra.com

ALLSTEEL

PRODUCT Benching system
COLLECTION Stride
www.allsteel.com

HALCON

PRODUCT Proximus
DESIGN David Grout and
Donna Corbat for Gary Lee Studios
www.halconcorp.com

TUOHY FURNITURE

PRODUCT Modular casegoods
COLLECTION Prato
www.tuohyfurniture.com

ICF GROUP

PRODUCT Mobi mobile workstation
DESIGN Andrea Ruggiero
www.icfgroup.com

EDESK

PRODUCT East Village
COLLECTION David Austin
DESIGN David Austin Murray
www.edesk.us

STEELCASE

PRODUCT FrameOne
www.steelcase.com

KNOLL

PRODUCT Desks, tables, storage, and screens
COLLECTION Antenna Workspaces
DESIGN Masamichi Udagawa
and Sigi Moeslinger
www.knoll.com

BERNHARDT DESIGN

PRODUCT Curio
DESIGN Claudia and Harry Washington

www.bernhardt.com

DAVIS FURNITURE

PRODUCT Tables, benches, and storage
COLLECTION Site

www.davisfurniture.com

NUCRAFT FURNITURE

PRODUCT Arena
DESIGN Mark Goetz

www.nucraft.com

TUOHY FURNITURE

PRODUCT Cubist conference table

www.tuohyfurniture.com

MOLTENI & C

PRODUCT Arc
DESIGNER Foster + Partners
www.moltenidada.com

PHILLIPS COLLECTION

PRODUCT River Stone
DESIGN Jason Phillips

www.phillipscollection.com

NOVA STUDIO INTERNATIONAL

PRODUCT Per Par Pum stackable chair-tables
DESIGN Lema

www.lemausa.com

SANDBACK

PRODUCT Drum
DESIGN Peter Sandback

www.petersandback.com

DARC
Design & Architecture

HONOREE FURNITURE / RESIDENTIAL STORAGE

Symmetry is for softies; Brancusi, for the bold. This dynamic
and multipurpose cabinet is an amalgam of five components
held aloft by a polished-stainless-steel base. Inside the large
square module, five drawers equipped with silent self-close
mechanisms glide on hidden runners. The two vertical pieces
are fitted with shelves, while the end-unit fronts are left open.
The 7-foot-wide cabinet can be dressed in Macassar ebony
or a host of alternate veneers: olivewood, *pao ferro*, zebrano,
walnut, and rosewood.

PRODUCT Brancusi
DESIGN Fermin Verdeguer
www.darc.es

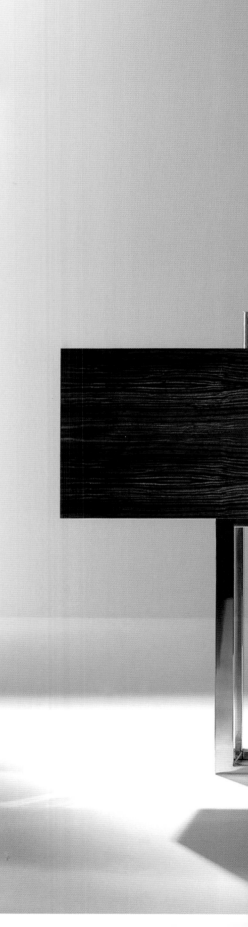

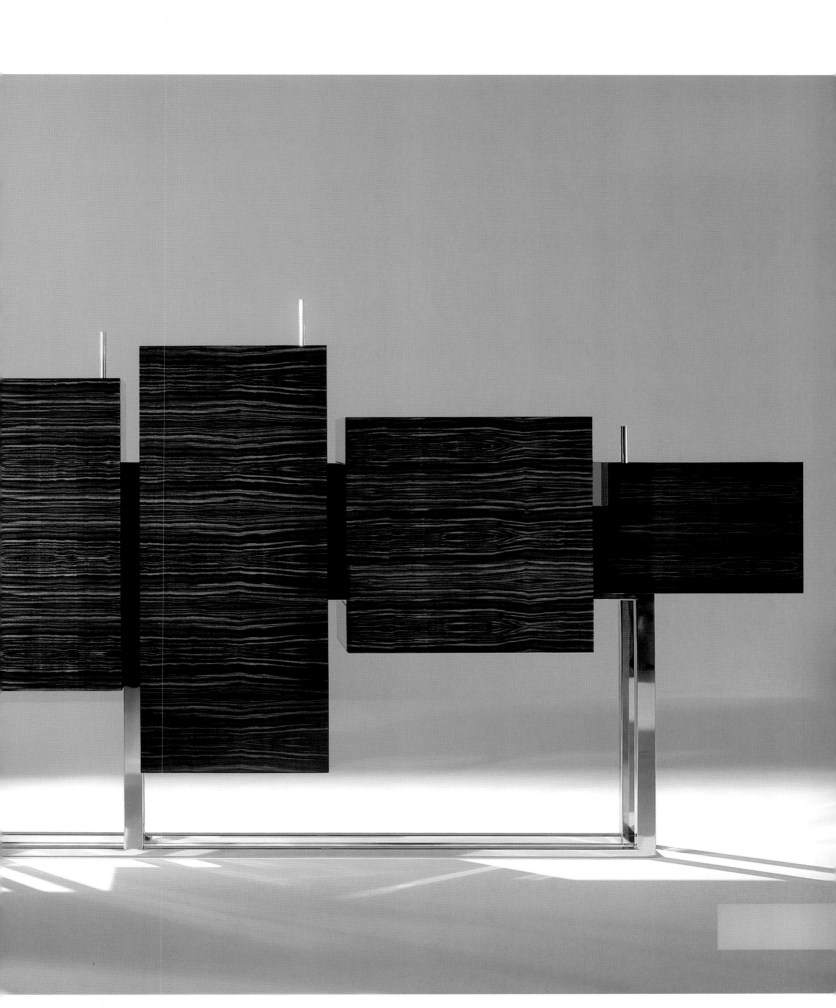

Clockwise from right:
Gianfranco Zaccai,
cofounder of design
firm Compass,
conceived the
modular system,
which can be
configured for a
variety of applica-
tions, such as exam
rooms. The modules
hang from wall-
mounted rails that
accommodate
structural imperfec-
tions and float
furnishings above
floors for easy
cleaning. ➤

Herman Miller

WINNER **FURNITURE / HEALTH CARE**

Advances in health care frequently trigger new
requirements and standards in hospital interiors.
This system anticipates such evolving needs with an
assortment of elements that are easy to assemble,
rearrange, and remove. Walls, storage units, work
surfaces, and accessories can be configured in a variety
of applications for patient rooms, surgery rooms, and
other clinical spaces. Components come covered in a
range of Corian options or low-PVC Durawrap polymer-
carbon composites that create seamless, cleanable
surfaces.

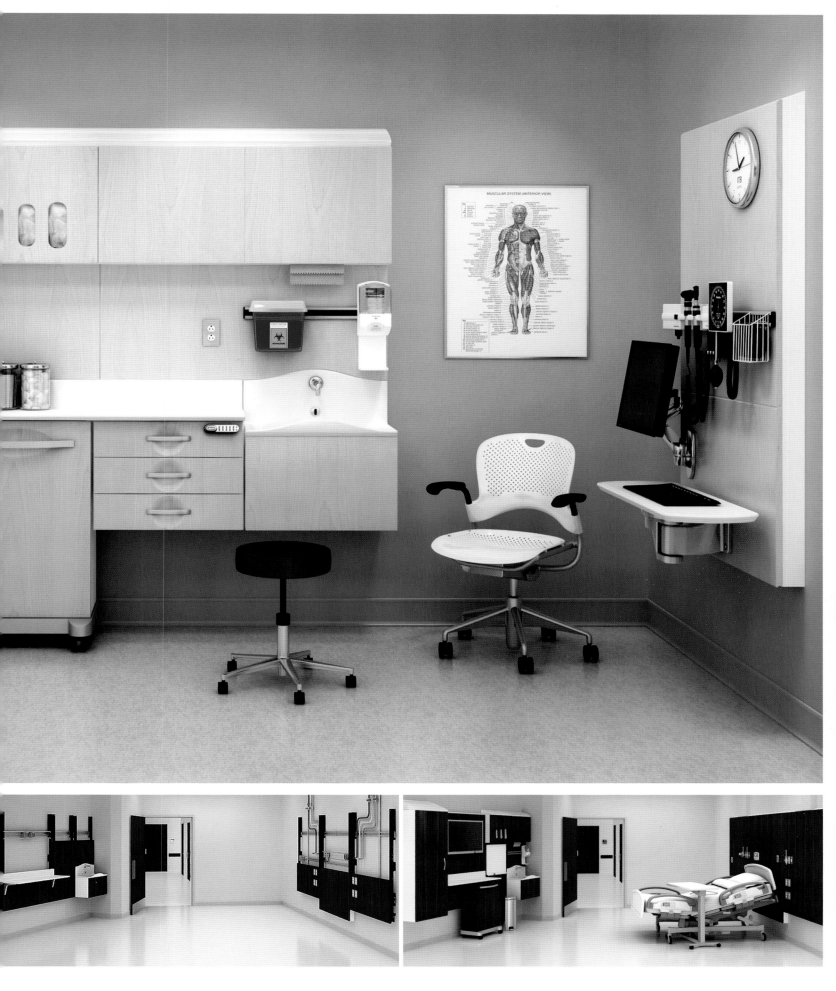

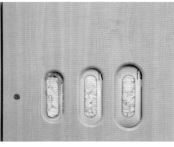

PRODUCT Walls, storage units, work surfaces, and accessories
COLLECTION Compass system
DESIGN Gianfranco Zaccai
www.hermanmiller.com/healthcare

Arcadia

HONOREE FURNITURE / HEALTH CARE

Today's healing environments demand equal doses of style and substance. Haven, a spry suite of seating and tables, easily meets the challenge. An antimicrobial finish shields the smooth and slender beech frame of the lounge chair, which features a passive flex back for long-term comfort (it's also available fully upholstered). Replaceable arm caps in wood or black urethane are generously proportioned to provide maximum stability. Optional add-ons include flip-up or rotating tablets, casters, and power trays.

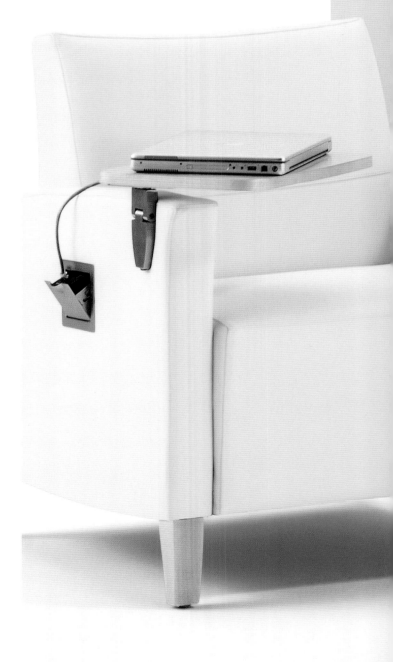

PRODUCT Seating and occasional tables
COLLECTION Haven
DESIGN David Dahl
www.arcadiacontract.com

Resource Furniture

WINNER FURNITURE / RESIDENTIAL STORAGE

Dorm rooms aren't the only places where sleeping and working need to coexist. Families with school-age kids often desire such an arrangement, but square footage—and a good-looking solution—are scarce. The PoppiBoard space-saving system combines a 24-inch-deep wardrobe with a twin wall bed and generously sized desk, creating an efficient, multi-function unit that's decidedly attractive—and clever. When it's time to shut the computer and grab some sleep, a patented mechanism keeps the desk surface level as you make the switch, eliminating the need to clear everything off first. Plus, your work will be there just as you left it when you wake up.

PRODUCT PoppiBoard space-saving system
DESIGN Clei
www.resourcefurniture.com

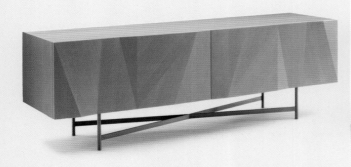

DUNE

PRODUCT Sierra low cabinet
DESIGN Claesson Koivisto Rune

www.dune-ny.com

POLIFORM

PRODUCT Skip bookcase system
DESIGN Studio Kairos

www.poliformusa.com

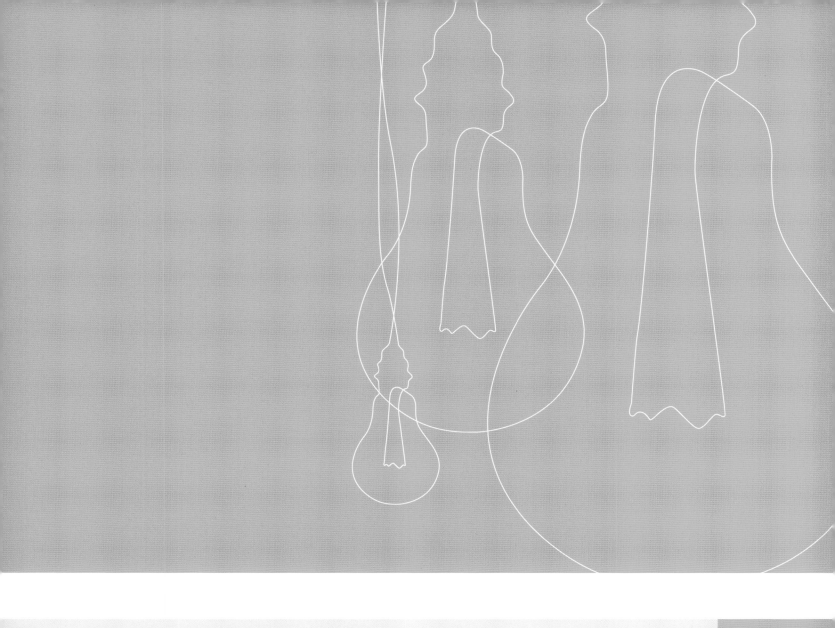

WIELAND

PRODUCT Allay sleep sofa

www.wielandhealthcare.com

PETER PEPPER PRODUCTS

PRODUCT Evolution modular wall system

www.peterpepper.com

VONDOM
PRODUCT Surf chaise
DESIGN Karim Rashid
www.vondom.com

HONOREES **FURNITURE** / **OUTDOOR LOUNGE**

ROYAL BOTANIA
PRODUCT D-Lux lounge chair
DESIGN Kris Van Puyvelde
www.royalbotania.com

JANUS ET CIE
PRODUCT Trennza
www.janusetcie.com

SUTHERLAND
PRODUCT Great Lakes chaise
DESIGN Terry Hunziker
www.davidsutherlandshowroom.com

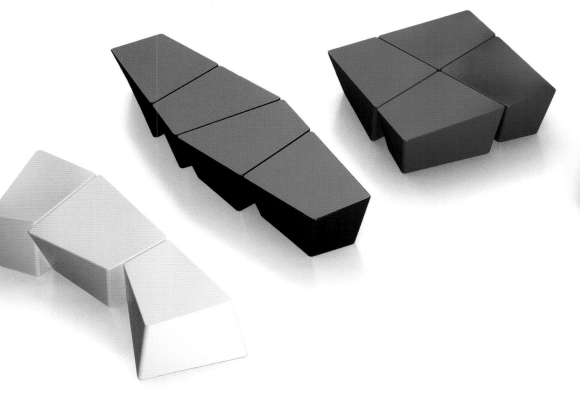

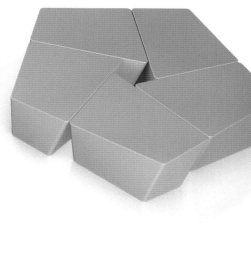

ITOKI DESIGN

PRODUCT CH bench
DESIGN Jeff Miller
www.itokidesign.com

RICHARD SHULTZ

PRODUCT Fresh Air dining chair
www.richardschultz.com

LANDSCAPE FORMS

PRODUCT Rest bench
COLLECTION Metro40
DESIGN BMW Group Design-works USA
www.landscapeforms.com

NEOTERIC LUXURY

PRODUCT Sphere swing
www.neotericluxury.com

ROCKY MOUNTAIN HARDWARE

COLLECTION Shift
DESIGN Ted Boerner

www.rockymountainhardware.com

HONOREES **HARDWARE**

TURNSTYLE DESIGNS

PRODUCT Door levers and pulls
COLLECTION Woven Leather

www.turnstyledesigns.com

SA BAXTER

COLLECTION Flute
DESIGN Robert A.M. Stern

www.sabaxter.com

SARGENT

PRODUCT 8200 mortise lock
with push/pull trim

www.sargentlock.com

U-LINE

PRODUCT 2175RCG glass-door
under-counter refrigerator
www.u-line.com

MIELE

PRODUCT Lumen ventilation hood with LED band
www.mieleusa.com

BULTHAUP

PRODUCT Air extractor
with wing slats
DESIGN EOOS
www.bulthaup.com

ELICA

PRODUCT Chrome hood
www.elica.com

DORNBRACHT

PRODUCT Lot water dispenser
DESIGN Sieger Design
www.dornbracht.com

HONOREES **KITCHEN FITTINGS**

SHOWHOUSE

PRODUCT Modern pot filler
www.moen.com

BRIZO

PRODUCT Venuto kitchen faucet with SmartTouch technology
www.brizo.com

BLANCO

PRODUCT Ronis sink
www.blancoamerica.com

ELKAY

PRODUCT Cascade compact sink
COLLECTION Design Inspirations
DESIGN Fu-Tung Cheng
www.elkay.com

LENOVA

PRODUCT Entertainer bar sink
www.lenovasinks.com

DURAVIT

PRODUCT Console
COLLECTION PuraVida
DESIGN Phoenix Design
www.duravit.com

KOHLER CO.

COLLECTION Robern wall-hung bathroom vanities
www.kohler.com

HENRYBUILT
PRODUCT Bar Block
www.henrybuilt.com

POGGENPOHL
COLLECTION +Artesio
DESIGN Hadi Teherani
www.poggenpohl.com

BULTHAUP
PRODUCT S cabinets with pocket-door mechanism
COLLECTION B3
www.bulthaup.com

TWISTER SCONE

PATTERN BLACK NIMBUS

And Bob's Your Uncle Lighting

HONOREE LIGHTING / PENDANT

Crystal chandeliers have become a design check mark of sorts: lovely, sure, but no longer an unexpected delight. ABYU Lighting aims high: sky-high, in fact. Parakeet Dome, which draws inspiration from cloud formations and birds, is the evolutionary successor to a lamp that designer Steven Wine first dreamed up for a photo shoot. Twister is an elegant tornado of light and feathers frozen in time. And the iridescent Pattern Black Nimbus evokes its namesake in rhinestones and crystals. Each flight of fancy is made by hand in the company's Manhattan workshop, where a team of artists employs millinery techniques in applying feathers to silk shades. Look up and be wowed.

PRODUCT Parakeet Dome pendant, Twister table sconce and lamp, and Pattern Black Nimbus pendant
DESIGN Steven Wine
www.abyulighting.com

PARAKEET DOME

TWISTER TABLE LAMP

BOCCI

PRODUCT Series 28 chandelier
DESIGN Omer Arbel
www.bocci.ca

HONOREES **LIGHTING** / **PENDANT**

SEGUSO

PRODUCT Canneto chandelier
www.seguso.com

ESTILUZ

PRODUCT Infiore pendant
DESIGN Lagranja
www.estiluz.com

KENTFIELD COLLECTION

PRODUCT On the Rocks sconce
DESIGN Sherry Williamson
www.kentfieldcollection.com

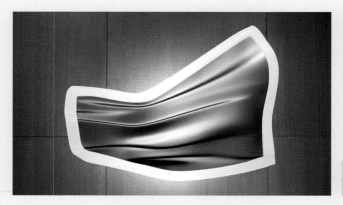

IVALO LIGHTING

PRODUCT Inflection LED interior sconce
www.ivalolighting.com

HUMANSCALE

PRODUCT Horizon LED task light
www.humanscale.com

VIBIA

PRODUCT Alpha bedside reading light
www.vibialight.com

From left: Zebrano is among the custom wood options offered. Available treatments also include custom metal grilles backed by Xorel fabric. ➤

Modernfold

HONOREE PARTITION & WALL SYSTEM

The periodic need to divvy up large spaces has too often resulted in moveable partitions that are functional yet bland, with a kind of high-school-gym vibe. Modernfold's operable walls give the category a real shot in the arm. Because of reciprocal agreements with various material providers—Chemetal, Interlam, Lumicor, and 3form among them—the brand can offer a host of exciting finishes and skins like stainless steel, laminate, and carpeting. The Designer line of Acousti-Seal partitions can also be customized on site to include framed glass, windows, and millwork. Spice up that ballroom, modular office, church...or even gymnasium. ➤

Clockwise from left:
Modernfold's Acousti-Seal design can be faced with textured laminates such as this one from Interlam's Art Diffusion line. Boston's Park Street church celebrated its 200-year anniversary with exterior restorations and an interior redesign incorporating Modernfold products. The church's welcome center can be subdivided courtesy of Designer Line partitions. Integrated windows and doors enhance functionality. A wood-trimmed tufted-leather version is ideal for hospitality and corporate environments alike.

PRODUCT Designer Line operable partitions
www.modernfold.com

Sancal

HONOREE SEATING / CONTRACT LOUNGE

The Tea collection, by José Manuel Ferrero of Spain's Estudihac Jmferrero, aims to arouse emotions in the user via sight and touch. Its name comes from the designer's inspiration—teatime and, in particular, an old tea set. But there's nothing stodgy about this service. The solid and two-tone chairs, armchairs, and sofas combine textures and materials with aplomb. Quilted matte velvet seats in sober colors and patterned hexagons reference traditional tweeds; the palette ranges from neutrals to maroon, green, and copper. It's a highly evolved play on mix and match, providing delightfully modern perches for impromptu meetings—or an afternoon cuppa.

COLLECTION Tea
DESIGN José Manuel Ferrero
www.sancal.com

3FORM
PRODUCT Ponder panels
COLLECTION Full Circle
www.3-form.com

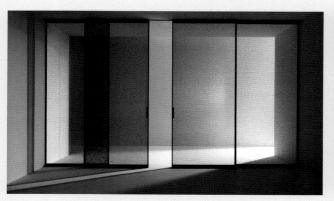

NOVA STUDIO INTERNATIONAL
PRODUCT Pavilion Minimal sliding-door frames with Penelope glass
COLLECTION Tre-P & Tre-Piu
DESIGN Antonio Citterio
www.novastudio.com

HAWORTH
PRODUCT Enclose frameless glass
www.haworth.com

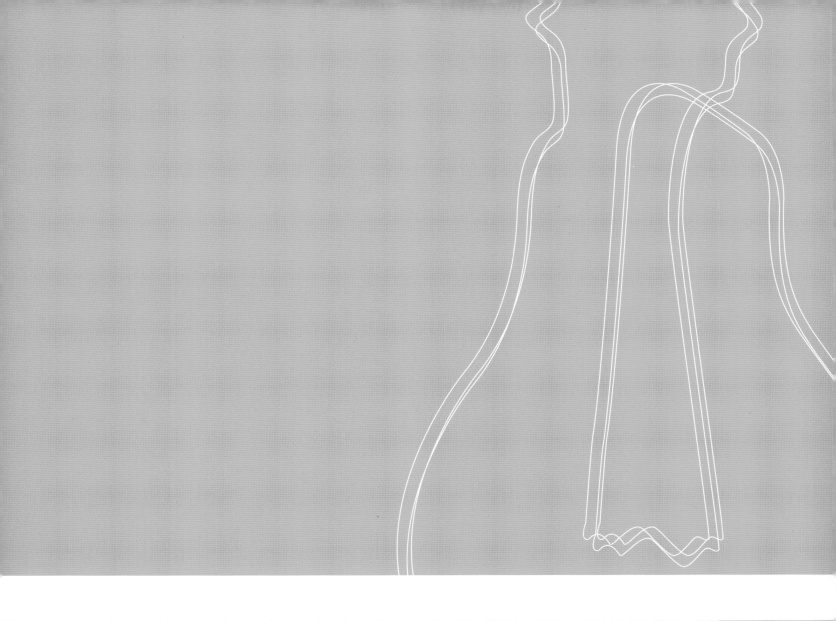

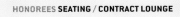

LOEWENSTEIN

COLLECTION Stryde
DESIGN Michael Wolk

www.ofsbrands.com

TEKNION

PRODUCT DNA modular seating
DESIGN Acer Design

www.teknion.com

DAUPHIN

PRODUCT Perillo
DESIGN Martin Ballendat

www.dauphin.com

DAVID EDWARD

PRODUCT Stern executive chair
DESIGN Robert A.M. Stern

www.davidedward.com

HONOREES **SEATING / CONTRACT CONFERENCE**

KNOLL

PRODUCT MultiGeneration
DESIGN Formway Design

www.knoll.com

STYLEX

PRODUCT Sava
DESIGN Sava Cvek

www.stylexseating.com

HAWORTH

PRODUCT Very

www.haworth.com

DUNE

PRODUCT Pipeline
DESIGN Harry Allen
www.dune-ny.com

BERNHARDT DESIGN

PRODUCT Corvo
DESIGN Noé Duchaufour-Lawrance
www.bernhardt.com

DAVID EDWARD

PRODUCT Aspen
DESIGN Scott Mason
www.davidedward.com

GEIGER INTERNATIONAL

PRODUCT Full Twist
www.geigerintl.com

STEELCASE
PRODUCT Node
www.steelcase.com

HONOREES **SEATING** / **CONTRACT TASK**

VITRA
PRODUCT Skape
DESIGN Antonio Citterio
www.vitra.com

HAWORTH
PRODUCT Very
www.haworth.com

STYLEX
PRODUCT Sava
DESIGN Sava Cvek
www.stylexseating.com

CABOT WRENN

PRODUCT Pratt Institute
DESIGN Students and faculty
www.cabotwrenn.com

EMECO

PRODUCT 111 Navy
www.emeco.net

NUSA FURNITURE

PRODUCT Tiburon
DESIGN Richard Patterson
of Clay and Wood
www.nusafurniture.com

BAKER FURNITURE

PRODUCT Pacquebot
COLLECTION André Arbus
www.baker.kohlerinteriors.com

DESIGN WITHIN REACH
COLLECTION Raleigh
www.dwr.com

HONOREES SEATING / **RESIDENTIAL LOUNGE**

VITRA
COLLECTION Suita
DESIGN Antonio Citterio
www.vitra.com

DUNE
COLLECTION Rebel
DESIGN Richard Shemtov
www.dune-ny.com

M2L
COLLECTION Gabo
DESIGN FSM
www.m2lcollection.com

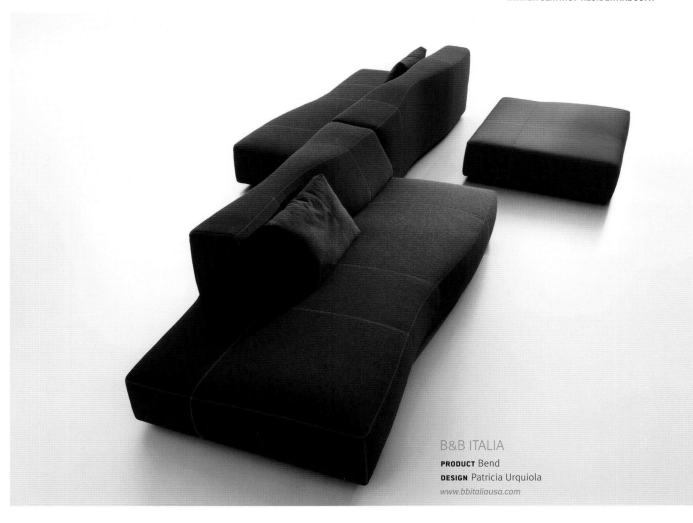

B&B ITALIA

PRODUCT Bend
DESIGN Patricia Urquiola
www.bbitaliausa.com

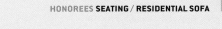

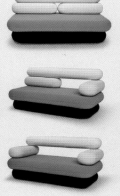

JANE HAMLEY WELLS

PRODUCT ADN
DESIGN Ramón Esteve
www.janehamleywells.com

DOMODINAMICA

PRODUCT Hot Dog
DESIGN Karim Rashid
www.domodinamica.com

DAVID EDWARD

PRODUCT Tulip
DESIGN Andrew Gower
www.davidedward.com

Momentum Group

HONOREE TEXTILES / CONTRACT

Sara Balderi mined the relationship between architecture and illumination to create her Through Light and Shadow collection of cotton-nylon blends. Flux captures the intermittent glimmer of city lights. Juncture plays off the hard-edge geometry of windowpanes and the shadows cast through them. And Revolve sports circles scored with energetic lines. All three boast Crypton InCase to thwart any soil, odor, or microbe.

PRODUCT Flux, Juncture, and Revolve
COLLECTION Through Light and Shadow
DESIGN Sara Balderi
www.themomgroup.com

REVOLVE

REVOLVE

FLUX

JUNCTURE

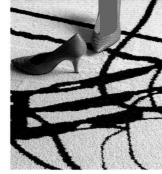

Crypton

HONOREE TEXTILES / HOSPITALITY

Creative types ordinarily eschew barriers, but in Power Lines, artist Randy Twaddle embraces them: The manufacturer's patented fiber-guarding technology provides an impermeable obstacle to stains, odor, and microbial matter. Once confined to the world of fabrics—80 million yards and counting—the treatment now provides protection to carpets, leather, and wall coverings. Thus the painterly splatter linking this coordinated series of textiles and carpeting is the only splash that stays behind.

PRODUCT Fabric, carpet, leather, and wall coverings
COLLECTION Power Lines
DESIGN Randy Twaddle
www.cryptonfabric.com

LUNA TEXTILES

PRODUCT Aspect and Facet
COLLECTION Dimensions
www.lunatextiles.com

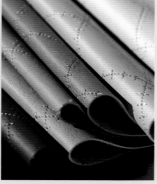

POLLACK

PRODUCT Geode
www.pollackassociates.com

JOSEPH NOBLE

PRODUCT Frankenstein
COLLECTION Technology Leather
www.josephnoble.com

EDELMAN LEATHER

COLLECTION Croco Loco

www.edelmanleather.com

GRETCHEN BELLINGER

PRODUCT Go for Baroque sequin lace

www.gretchenbellinger.com

LUNA TEXTILES

PRODUCT Dots Damask and Mobile

COLLECTION Kinetic

www.lunatextiles.com

BERGAMO FABRICS

PRODUCT Orchidea
COLLECTION Sahco Ulf Moritz

www.bergamofabrics.com

HONOREES **TEXTILES** / **RESIDENTIAL**

S. HARRIS

COLLECTION Amy Lau for S. Harris
DESIGN Amy Lau

www.sharris.com

DONGHIA

PRODUCT Shibori Stripe
COLLECTION Donghia Textiles

www.donghia.com

KRAVET

COLLECTION Thom Filicia
for Kravet Collections
DESIGN Thom Filicia

www.kravet.com

CF STINSON

COLLECTION Jazz
DESIGN Jane Wicks
www.cfstinson.com

ARCHITEX

COLLECTION Remede
www.architex-ljh.com

ROBERT ALLEN CONTRACT

COLLECTION DwellStudio
for Robert Allen Contract
Healthcare Collection
DESIGN DwellStudio
www.robertallendesign.com

PALLAS TEXTILES

COLLECTION Entwined
DESIGN Laura Guido-Clark
www.pallastextiles.com

SINA PEARSON
TEXILES

PRODUCT Flora, Poncho, and Serape
COLLECTION Colores de Mexico
www.sinapearson.com

HONOREES **TEXTILES / OUTDOOR**

JOSEPH NOBLE

COLLECTION Plastic: Rubber
www.josephnoble.com

ALAXI FABRICS

COLLECTION Improv
www.alaxifabrics.com

PERENNIALS
OUTDOOR FABRICS

COLLECTION More Amore
www.perennialsfabrics.com

DESIGNTEX

PRODUCT Xeriscape
COLLECTION Rinekwall
for Designtex
DESIGN Rinekwall
www.designtex.com

BART HALPERN

COLLECTION Glitterati

www.barthalpern.com

NEW RAVENNA MOSAICS

PRODUCT Octopus Garden
glass mosaics

www.newravenna.com

PHILLIP JEFFRIES

COLLECTION Lacquered Strié

www.phillipjeffries.com

Maya Romanoff

WINNER WALL COVERING / RESIDENTIAL

Maya Romanoff's fixation on tie-dye was sparked at Woodstock '69, the very same year the designer launched his signature line. Fast-forward four decades and his eponymous company is the go-to source for exceptional wall coverings. To mark its 40-year milestone, the brand developed an Anniversary collection, for which designer Amy Lau updated three archival patterns. Half Plaid has horizontal pleats, Snowflake recalls a stained-glass star, and Crystal conjures the view from within its namesake mineral. All papers are hand-dyed using lustrous water-based pigments. How groovy is that? ➤

PARAVENT

HALF PLAID

CRYSTAL

SNOWFLAKE

HALF PLAID

Clockwise from left:
The Anniversary collection's Half Plaid wallpaper pattern in a living room application. Maya Romanoff, newly resplendent in tie-dyes discovered at 1969's Woodstock music festival. Romanoff in 2009. Chicago's Sun-Times Building in 1996, which Romanoff covered in 120-foot-long banners of hand-dyed cotton canvas. Amy Lau reinvented a 1976 tie-dyed textile as the Anniversary collection's Snowflake.

PRODUCT Crystal, Half Plaid, and Snowflake
COLLECTION Anniversary
DESIGN Amy Lau
www.mayaromanoff.com

WINNER WALL COVERING / RESIDENTIAL

Hunter Douglas

HONOREE WINDOW TREATMENT

Traditional window treatments can look clumsy and out of place in contemporary settings, like a poorly trained butler. Thankfully, Hunter Douglas has figured out how to get the effect of tailored drapes and sheers without the bulk, marrying the elements on a single headrail. The fixed "drapery" portion consists of a woven fabric, with vanes that provide structure, resulting in smooth, uniform columns. Center-opening or side-stack sheers are knit panels—bonded to vanes—that rotate for privacy control and diffuse incoming sunlight. What a bright idea.

PRODUCT Luminette Modern Draperies Dual Panel
www.hunterdouglas.com

WOLF-GORDON

PRODUCT Glow, Swarovski Crystals; Sparkle,
Swarovski Crystals; and Stars, Swarovski Crystals

www.wolf-gordon.com

GRAHAM & BROWN

PRODUCT Lacework
DESIGN Amy Butler

www.grahambrownusa.com

WEITZNER

PRODUCT Newsworthy
COLLECTION Apropos
DESIGN Lori Weitzner

www.loriweitzner.com

HUNTER DOUGLAS
CONTRACT

PRODUCT RB 500
roller-shade system
www.hunterdouglascontract.com

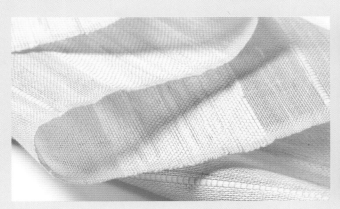

CONRAD

PRODUCT Weave No. 1738 Caprice
www.conradshades.com

LUTRON ELECTRONICS CO.

PRODUCT Kirbé vertical drapery system
www.lutron.com

ANN SACKS

PRODUCT Indah wood tile
www.annsacks.com

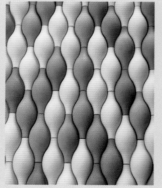

DESIGNTEX

PRODUCT WriteUp H2O dry-erase coating
www.designtex.com

URBAN ARCHAEOLOGY

PRODUCT Push Pull
COLLECTION Revolv
www.urbanarchaeology.com

PORCELANOSA

PRODUCT Qatar tile
www.porcelanosa-usa.com

PETER AARON / ESTO
www.esto.com

JOHN ABERNATHY
www.abernathyphoto.com

GEORGE APOSTOLIDIS
www.georgeapostolidis.com

TOM ARBAN
www.tomarban.com

FARSHID ASSASSI
www.assassi.com

LINCOLN BARBOUR
www.lincolnbarbour.com

CHRISTOPHER BARRETT
www.christopherbarrett.net

BENJAMIN BENSCHNEIDER
www.benschneiderphoto.com

ANTOINE BOOTZ
www.antoinebootz.com

RICHARD BRYANT / ARCAID
www.arcaid.co.uk

BENNY CHAN / FOTOWORKS
www.fotoworks.cc

BASIL CHILDERS
www.basilphoto.com

RON COOPER
www.roncooperphotography.com

BRUCE DAMONTE
www.brucedamonte.com

EVAN DION
www.evandion.com

JESSE DITTMAR
www.jessedittmar.com

JÜRGEN EHEIM
www.eheim.it

JOHN ELLIS
www.johnellisphoto.com

LEONARDO FINOTTI
www.leonardofinotti.com

ELIZABETH FRAIBERG / E3 PHOTOGRAPHY
www.photographye3.com

SCOTT FRANCES
www.scottfrances.com

AMIT GERON
www.amitgeron.com

SHAI GIL
www.shaigil.com

PAUL GOSNEY
www.paulgosney.com

ART GRAY
www.artgrayphotography.com

best of year photographers

TIM GRIFFITH
www.timgriffith.com

KEN HAYDEN
www.kenhayden.com

EDWARD HENDRICKS / CI&A PHOTOGRAPHY
www.ciaphoto.com.sg

GREGORY HOLM
www.gregoryholm.com

EDUARD HUEBER / ARCH PHOTO
www.archphoto.com

TIMOTHY HURSLEY
www.timothyhursley.com

NATHAN KIRKMAN
www.nathankirkman.com

NIKOLAS KOENIG
www.nikolaskoenig.com

NELSON KON
www2.nelsonkon.com.br

ERIC LAIGNEL
www.ericlaignel.com

DAVID LENA
www.lenaphoto.com

PETER MAUSS / ESTO
www.esto.com

SCOTT MAYORAL
www.mayoralphoto.com

SCOTT McDONALD / HEDRICH BLESSING
www.hedrichblessing.com

SHANNON McGRATH
www.shannonmcgrath.com

TOM McWILLIAM
www.tommcwilliam.com

DERRYCK MENERE
www.derryckmenere.com

MATTHEW MILLMAN
www.matthewmillman.com

MICHAEL MORAN
www.moranstudio.com

OLAF MUELLER
www.omstudio.hk

PETER MURDOCK
www.petermurdock.com

JAIME NAVARRO
www.jaimenavarrophotographer.com

TOM OLCOTT
www.tgolcott.com

PEDRO PEGENAUTE
www.pedropegenaute.es

TOM POWEL
www.tompowelimaging.com

KEN PROBST
www.kennethprobst.com

UNDINE PRÖHL
www.undineprohl.com

BEN RAHN / A-FRAME
www.aframestudio.ca

RICKY RIDECÓS
www.rickyridecos.com

MICHAEL DAVID ROSE
www.mdrp.net

DURSTON SAYLOR
www.durstonsaylor.com

BOONE SPEED
www.boonespeed.com

BRANKO STARCEVIC
www.brankostarcevic.com

BRAD STEIN
www.bradstein.com

ERIC STRIFFLER
www.striffler.com

TIMMERMAN PHOTOGRAPHY
www.billtimmerman.com

DAVID WAKELY
www.davidwakely.com

PAUL WARCHOL
www.warcholphotography.com

MATT WINQUIST
www.winquistphotography.com

INTERIOR DESIGN®

editor in chief Cindy Allen

EXECUTIVE EDITOR
Elena Kornbluth

DEPUTY EDITOR
Edie Cohen (West/Southwest)

ARTICLES EDITOR
Annie Block

SENIOR EDITORS
Mark McMenamin
Deborah Wilk

MANAGING EDITOR
Helene E. Oberman

ASSOCIATE EDITOR
Meghan Edwards

DESIGNERS
Zigeng Li
Karla Lima
Giannina Macias

BOOKS EDITOR
Stanley Abercrombie

EDITOR AT LARGE
Craig Kellogg

MARKET EDITOR AT LARGE
Karen D. Singh

CONTRIBUTING EDITORS
Aric Chen
Cindy Coleman
Laura Fisher Kaiser
Nicholas Tamarin

PRODUCTION MANAGER
Jessica Perrin / 646-938-9199 / jperrin@interiordesign.net

PRODUCTION COORDINATOR
Sarah Dentry / 646-805-0236 / sdentry@interiordesign.net

DIGITAL IMAGING
Igor Tsiperson

RESEARCH DIRECTOR
Wing Leung / 646-805-0250

REPRINTS
Ness Feliciano / 708-660-8612 / fax 708-660-8613

INTERIORDESIGN.NET
WEB EDITOR
Laurel Petriello

DESIGNWIRE DAILY CONTRIBUTORS
Sheila Kim
Ghislaine Viñas
Ian Volner
Larry Weinberg

SANDOW|MEDIA™

Chairman and CEO of Sandow Media Adam I. Sandow

CHIEF FINANCIAL OFFICER AND CHIEF OPERATING OFFICER
Chris Fabian

VICE PRESIDENT, CREATIVE AND EDITORIAL
Yolanda E. Yoh

VICE PRESIDENT, INFORMATION TECHNOLOGY
Tom Cooper

president Mark Strauss, hon. iida

ASSOCIATE PUBLISHER
Carol Cisco

DIGITAL MEDIA DIRECTOR
Carrie Knoblock

STRATEGIC AD DIRECTOR, NEW YORK
Gayle Shand

MARKETING DIRECTOR
Tina Brennan

PROJECTS DIRECTOR, ASSISTANT TO THE PRESIDENT
Hae Soo Kim

MARKETING
ART DIRECTOR
Denise Figueroa

SENIOR DESIGNER
Mihoko Miyata

ASSOCIATE MANAGER
Yasmin Spiro / 646-805-2087

INTERIORDESIGN.NET
DIGITAL MEDIA MANAGER
Ashley Walker

AD SERVICES COORDINATOR
Nicole Dziamba

GO-TO BUYERS GUIDE PRODUCER
Eric Perl

SERVICES
HALL OF FAME DIRECTOR
Regina Freedman / 646-805-0270

CONTRACTS COORDINATOR
Sandy Campomanes / 646-805-0403

SPECIAL PROJECTS MANAGER
Kay Kojima / 646-805-0276

SALES
SALES REPRESENTATIVE
Kathy Harrigan / 646-805-0292

INTEGRATED MEDIA SALES
Karen Donaghy / 646-805-0291

INSIDE SALES DIRECTOR
Jonathan Kessler / 646-805-0279

INSIDE SALES REPRESENTATIVE
Danielle Whiteman / 646-805-0278

SALES ASSOCIATE
Xiang Ping Zhu / 646-805-0269

SENIOR SALES COORDINATOR
Valentin Ortolaza / 646-805-0268

SALES ASSISTANT
Ashley Teater / 646-805-0271

PHILADELPHIA
Greg Kammerer / 610-738-7011 / fax 610-738-7195

ATLANTA BUYERS GUIDE, E-SALES MANAGER
Craig Malcolm / 770-712-9245 / fax 770-234-5847

CHICAGO
Tim Kedzuch / 847-907-4050 / fax 847-556-6513
Julie McCarthy / 847-615-2077 / fax 847-713-4897

LOS ANGELES
Reed Fry / 949-223-1088 / fax 949-223-1089

FRANCE/GERMANY/POLAND
Mirek Kraczkowsk / kraczko@aol.com / 48-22-401-7001 / fax 48-22-401-7016

ITALY
Riccardo Laureri / media@laureriassociates.it / 39-02-236-2500 / fax 39-02-236-4411

ASIA
Quentin Chan / quentinchan@leadingm.com / 852-2366-1106 / fax 852-2366-1107

AUDIENCE MARKETING SENIOR DIRECTOR
Katharine Tucker